TAKE YOUR PLACE!

Equipping Men to Lead In The 21st Century

THE HOUSE THAT COLE BUILT - REVISED

By G.F. Watkins

PRESS

www.xulonpress.com

To Rose

ENDORSEMENTS

This is a book written by a man who loves truth. His success resulted from teaching and practicing truth. He is a man who does not practice what he preaches but preaches what he practices.

One of his friends said," When opportunity appears, it is spelled W-O-R-K. Most people do not take advantage of opportunity, or are indifferent to it, because they don't want more work."

More work requires more commitment. Commitment requires the giving of self-living outside the "comfort zone" on the edge. But when all is said and done, the edge is the safest place because it's where God lives.

G.F. Watkins is a doer, not a talker. Dreaming without doing is foolishness, the proverb reads-so is reading without doing. This is a book for doers who read. Thank you G. F. for being a doer, for studying, practicing, writing and challenging men today.

Edwin Louis Cole
Founder and President
Christian Men's Network

Dr. Cole taught us that "When you accept another man's philosophy, you also accept that man's consequences for the philosophy." Never has it been truer than by the man who wrote this amazing book. Pastor GF Watkins accepted and embraced Dr. Cole's philosophy of life and as a result, is seeing the consequence of tremendous ministry and men's changed lives all over the world. Pastor GF carries the DNA of Dr. Cole's life, mentoring, friendship, and teaching. He is full of the truths that set men free. His example of honor and sonship with Dr. Cole gives a shining example of how we are to honor our spiritual fathers. This book will change your life because God's hand is on Pastor GF Watkins and His hand will be on you. Get ready to receive it!

Tony Rorie
Founder & Director,
Men of Honor & Ladies of Honor, Dallas, TX

A handbook for sons on how to pay tribute as a son & honor your father. This book personifies who Pastor GF is and what he does. The book is a challenge & call to real manhood, an understanding of the mandate given to be about our father's business. Every man must read this book to complete his circle of life, finish strong and pass the baton.

Carven Izaks
Sr. Pastor
Powerhouse Church Namibia, Africa

Spiritual fathers do not come into your life by way of anointing with oil and falling in the spirit. They come

vi

into your life by relationship as well as pursuit by the son. Some of the fortunate came into a relationship with Ed Cole and they are better men for it today.

Brother John Avanzini
Kerrville, Texas

"The pathway to greatness is found in this book, an incredible must read for those desiring to become real men.

How true that "unless a man proves faithful to what belongs to another he will not be qualified to have his own. Luke 16:12

Who else but a faithful son, can be qualified to reveal the secret keys to a father's wisdom on how to become a great man.

In this book, G.F. Watkins opens his heart to share priceless wisdom learned at the feet of his spiritual father/mentor the late, Edwin Louis Cole, also known as the founding father of the Men's Movement around the world.

I applaud the effort and time G.F. has taken to share the father's heart with us who are called to change the world.

Dr. Joaquin G. Molina
World Changer
Pastor/Author:
"Restoring the Gates that Prevail"

"The beauty of this book is that G.F. Watkins is not only talking about biblical principles and truths he learned from

Elijah, but he has put it together in a way that makes it a life-changing experience for the reader. I highly endorse G.F. Watkins, his commitment to Christ, and his love for making true disciples by turning Boy Scouts into true soldiers of the cross in this powerful army of God."

Pastor Mark Barclay
Founder and Pastor of Living Word International
Founder and President of Supernatural Ministries
Training Institute

I have known G.F. for 51 years and can attest to the fact that he can talk the talk because he has always walked the walk making me a proud father.

Gayle Watkins Jr.
Coach, principal, superintendent of schools. Father.

"Take Your Place."

"Those who stay will be champions!" That's the sign that hung over the locker room exit as we faced the challenges of another grueling University Of Southern California football practice. It was a quick gut-check to see what we were made of... What price were we willing to pay to be the best? In "Take your place," we see a book that will prove to be the ultimate spiritual bench mark in the life of any man or in the leadership of the local church. As children of God we are owners of nothing, yet stewards of everything! The greatest thing we must steward is our sphere of influence. G.F. Watkins gives men a creed to live by, a destiny to shoot for and a mission to accomplish! Through "Take Your Place", God is calling the men of this generation to get off the bench and make a difference in our society and culture. Learn it... Live it... Shake your world for Christ!

Tom (Big Tommy) Sirotnak
Former USC Defensive Team Captain
Founder: Sirotnak Evangelistic Network & Discipleship
(SEND)

GF Watkins in "Take Your Place" manages to teach us the essence of a man, as he wrote, "God cannot make an able man faithful, but He can make a faithful man able." You can now take your men from an unproductive group to highly effective team. This book is a must for pastors, church leaders and church workers.

Pastor Guillermo Aguayo
Mision Cristiana la Casa del Padre
Lima, Peru

"Dr. Cole's words of wisdom built my marriage, my ministry, and my house. Now those same foundation tools are available to you."

Pastor G.F. Watkins

ACKNOWLEDGEMENTS

Thanks to the men and women of Christian Men's Network who supported the ministry of Dr. Edwin Louis Cole with their time, talent, and treasure.

Thanks to my wife Rose and my sons, Cole, Grant, and Dayne, who allowed me to learn to be a father and husband, and support me in the process. They are my heroes!

Thanks to the men of PowerHouse Church for joining me in this great adventure to reverse the curse and restore order in a world of chaos.

Thanks to the women of PowerHouse for standing by me and the men of this church as we attempt to go where no man has gone before- to the land where being a male is a matter of birth but being a man is a matter of choice.

Thank you Dr. Ed Cole and family. You changed my life. You built my house. You helped me to "TAKE MY PLACE". I love you.

TABLE OF CONTENTS

FOREWORD

Ed Cole stands like a giant against the backdrop of a vital church history in the last third of the 20th century. I say "vital", because there's a vast difference between those churchmen who hold position and those who shape hearts, between those who gain social status and those who transform lives. The sheer impact of ministry, especially upon men, has left a stamp of "vital life" and will continue to effect change for generations by reason of those who, via Ed, have been changed by grace and for good.

The Bible says of David, "He served God in his generation," and thus reminds us of the fundamental stewardship to which each of us are accountable. It involves being discernibly sensitive to the spirit of our time, faithfully serving our sphere of influence for the duration of our given time, and so energetically discharging ourselves that a legacy is left in people who live beyond our time. This summarizes Ed's fidelity to his call and his faithful service of his God-given life-mission.

As a fellow servant in the Gospel, I was always encouraged by Ed's Godly manliness and righteous boldness in the Spirit of God and forthright prophetic stance in both his personal relationships, as well as his public declaration of God's Word of truth. As a young brother in Christ, I was personally blessed to feel his warm acceptance and supporting affirmation of my ministry, but I was also stirred to somehow always sense a summons, a call beyond on myself – a summons not always verbalized, but present and prodding me towards God's highest and best. It was infectious through Ed's way of living, speaking, and manifestly molding; it was Ed's way of leading. In everything about him, something breathed a fatherly word expressing the father's word, saying: *open to more than you thought you could become, because the Spirit has come to enable you to accomplish what the father always had in mind for you.*

Ed's home going was neither a disappointment to me, nor did I feel a loss. Why? First, because I felt that in knowing him I had touched the life of a man who ran every step of the race set before him and won, and there is no disappointment and watching a winner complete his course. Second, I felt no loss because the continuing force of the momentum set forward by his running is still igniting and moving us all – as it will continue to do so for years to come.

Ed Cole manifests the meaning of triumphing in Christ – and we have cause not only to rejoice in his life of vital victory, but we have been stimulated thereby more of that Christ-like vitality of our own.

Pastor Jack Hayford
Church on the Way
Van Nuys, California

A WORD ABOUT ED COLE

"There is a very interesting phenomenon occurring in America. From birth to late teens, a child's overwhelming perception of authority figures is nearly 100% female, with an occasional male making a generally ineffectual appearance.

In the hospital, female nurses are responsible for almost every aspect of childcare. At home, mother is usually the dominant authority figure. And 90% of the teachers in grade school are-you guessed it-women. The first police person a child meets is more than likely a female crossing guard.

When a child goes to the movies, grocery store, department stores, fast food restaurants, fancy sit down restaurants, vacation Bible school, or Sunday school, who is it that sells the tickets, takes the orders, collects the money, shows you where to sit, or tells you about God? (Except in many churches where a man preaches to a congregation consisting of mostly women.) Who tells you what to wear, to cleanup your room; who spends the money and pays the bills? In other words, who is really in charge? Is it any wonder that today's young man is making the very effort to demonstrate that he's a real man –like MOM.

So today's man may wear jewelry, bracelets, necklaces, and perhaps an earring. He has long hair and wears tight shirts opened to display "cleavage." Or he may be a macho man who acts irresponsibly with his wife and children or who indulges in sexual freedom and does his "own thing."

In any case man is "liberated." Or so he's been told by feminist principles, which undercut his position as a male.

At the same time, women are wearing shorter haircuts, masculine pants and suits, and in some case, neckties. In an attempt to assert their true selves or punish their oppressors, many women have allowed suppressed rage or self-hatred to erupt into violence against the men they perceive as being at fault.

Men and women not knowing exactly who they are or what their respective roles are, are confused and anxiety ridden.

Being a male is a matter of birth, being a man is a matter of choice. Thank you Lord for making us who we are. Thank you Ed for reminding us.

This was written in 1980 and though the wording has changed, the principles are still the same and manhood is still in trouble. Millions of these books have circulated the earth and set men free. I hope to illustrate what happens when we as men go beyond reading and shouting AMEN and actually begin to live these principles out.

From the "Foreword by Ben Kinchlow" of Maximized Manhood by Edwin Lewis Cole, © 1982, pp. xx–xx. Used by permission of Whitaker House (www.whitakerhouse.com). All rights reserved.

INTRODUCTION

"Everyone hold hands and makes a circle," Anna says to her Sunday school classroom full of five-year-olds. She's prepared all week to teach in the nursery and wanted to begin with a moment of prayer. "William, we'll start with you. What is your prayer request today?" As Mrs. Anna made her way around the circle, there are scratches that need healing, toys that need to be found, and older siblings that need to quit picking so much. When it was finally Sarah's turn to speak, her eyes began to well up with tears. "Sweetheart, what can we pray with you about today?" Anna asked. With tears visibly rolling down her cheeks, Sarah made her request, "Can you pray for my daddy to come back home?" The awkward silence was broken when Jason said, "Can you pray for my daddy to come home too?"

In America tonight, **one out of every three** children will go to bed in a home without their biological father. Our nation is suffering from a deadly plague. It's all around us, in the world and church alike. Fatherlessness is destroying the natural and spiritual immune system of our society, and the results are devastating. Research proves that children growing up in a fatherless home are:

- 5 times more likely to commit suicide (Source: US DHHS Bureau of the Census)
- 32 times more likely to run away (Source: US DHHS

Bureau of the Census)
- 20 times more likely to have behavioral disorders (Source: Center of Disease Control)
- 14 times more likely to commit rape (boys) (Source: Criminal Justice & Behavior, Vol. 14, p 403-26, 1978)
- 9 times more likely to drop out of school (Source: National Principles Association Report on the State of High Schools)
- 10 times more likely to abuse chemical substances (Source: Survey on Child Health, Washington, DC, 1993)
- 9 times more likely to end up in a state operation institution (Source: US Dept. of Justice Special Report, Sept, 1998)
- 20 times more likely to end up in prison (Source: Fulton Co. Georgia Jail Populations, Texas Department of Public Corrections, 1992)

While doctors, scientists, and psychologists frantically search for answers, God has already given us the ultimate remedy. Furthermore, His plan to reverse the curse is not a mere suggestion, but a **commandment**- if the father's hearts are not turned back to the children, a curse will overtake the Earth **(Malachi 4:6).**

As we identify the strategy to reverse the curse, we will explore the attributes of *spiritual fathers and sons*. I'll be sharing principles that my father in the faith, **Dr. Edwin Louis Cole**, and many others instilled in me. His mentorship revitalized my marriage, transformed my family, and liter-ally built my personal house, as well as my church home, PowerHouse Church. The memory of Dr. Ed Cole continues to challenge me to this very day to live a maximized life.

I want you to know that this book is not an attempt to make you a better family man, though being a family man is certainly a byproduct of becoming a spiritual father. **I'm writing to tell the world about the strategy God has given His people to heal our land.**

The discipleship plan contained in this book is a worldwide vision. It brings purpose and passion to men and hope and healing to women and children. This book is for leaders in search of answers, individuals looking for direction, and all those who are in need of a blueprint for the house (life) God created you to build. It's unique and only you hold the keys.

This book is for men and women who are trying to find fulfillment in life, and for fathers searching for the right words to give their children. It's for the multitudes that wake up every day and want more than anything to do something significant with their lives. This book is for little girls like Sarah who cry themselves to sleep wondering, "*Where is my father?*"

Sarah's answer, as well as yours, will be found within the next 17 chapters!

1

CHOICES

"Being a male is a matter of birth; being a man is a matter of choice."

It was a beautiful day in Newport Beach, California. I heard birds singing, the majestic ocean roaring, and yet my heart was heavy. On any other day, I would have marveled at the awesomeness of the blue sky, but on this day, it was all I could do to lift my head to the sun. It was September 6, 2002, and I watched them lower my hero into the ground.

Dr. Edwin Louis Cole was known to many as "the father of the Christian Men's Movement," but he felt more like "father" to me. Over the years, his character, convictions, and counsel lead me into the reality of my God-given purpose; now he was gone.

Since starting Christian Men's Network (C.M.N) in 1979, Dr. Cole's straightforward teachings and life-changing truths reached millions of men. C.M.N. birthed ministries in 210 nations. Over 4 million copies of Dr. Cole's books, written in more than forty languages, made their way into the hands and hearts of our generation. He relentlessly traveled the globe, reaching the masses through men's events, television, radio, retreats, books, and tapes, yet somehow, he always managed to make time for me. I owe my very manhood, marriage, and ministry to his mentorship.

I was not grieving alone. Hundreds of people came to Dr. Cole's funeral to pay respect to the man who chose to be just that – a man. It was an amazing sight to behold movie stars, dignitaries, ministers, and men and women from all walks of life share heartfelt stories of Dr. Cole's impact and influence on their life. We may have traveled from a diverse range of countries and cultures to be there that day, but we had one thing in common: we all wondered how we would go on without Dr. Cole, our Dad.

My mind was racing, not only with the reality of Dr. Cole's death, but with the invitation I had recently received. Just days before the funeral, Paul, Dr. Cole's son, asked me to speak at Dr. Cole's homegoing service at the Potter's House in Dallas, Texas. He told me that his father, in his last days of life, asked for three specific men to speak at his memorial service. Much to my surprise, I was one of them. I was humbled and honored Dr. Cole chose me, and I fervently asked God to give me the right words to say.

As I pondered the idea that my spiritual father was no longer a phone call away, I felt vulnerable, and yes, even insecure. Fathers are pillars of strength that we lean on throughout the many challenges and changes in life. Once they are gone, we must find the fortitude within ourselves to stand on our own.

Fathers are the pillars of strength we lean on throughout the many challenges and changes in life.

While I could not comprehend what my life was going to be like without Dr. Cole's stability and support, I was confident of one thing- his training and mentorship had equipped me for this new season of independence. Despite the anguish in my heart, I knew God has prepared me for "such a time as this". God placed Dr. Cole in my life for a far greater purpose than

I originally suspected. It was bigger than my marriage, my ministry, and my life. It was about winning God's man back and fulfilling God's purpose.

RESTORING DOMINION

Dr. Cole taught me that, "Being a male is matter of birth, being a man is a *matter of choice*." We choose to rise to the challenge of manhood and all that it entails. **God is the same yesterday, today, and forever (Hebrews 13:8),** and His mandate to men has not changed. What He expected from Adam, the first man, He expects from us today. Unfortunately, most men live their entire lives unaware of their divine purpose, with no plan to achieve true significance. I'm not just talking about the unsaved masses. There are pulpits full of men who faithfully prepare Sunday morning messages and all the

We choose to rise to the challenge of manhood and all that it entails.

while wonder, "Is this all there is?" While the congregation laughs at our jokes, on the inside we're crying out for inner fulfillment. It's not that we lack love or passion for God, it's that we have yet to discover what God wants us to do with that love and passion.

In **Genesis 1:28**, God told Adam to, **"Be fruitful and multiply; fill the earth and subdue it."** Now this passage is not as simple as, *"Have children and teach them to succeed in life."* This is actually a spiritual strategy to win God's man back, which is as effective today as it was in the very first generation of man. I want to break down the various aspects of this commission from God, because it's imperative that we understand our purpose and the plan. This Scripture explains both, and I believe it is a prophetic word for our generation.

First, God expects us to be *fruitful*. God wants our life

to be productive, not just in the natural, but in the Spirit. Success in God's kingdom always equates to souls, and redeemed lives are the fruit God desires. No matter what our specific calling is (pastor, Sunday school teacher, paymaster, etc.), we've all been charged with the mandate to win souls.

Coupled with the command to be fruitful is the command to multiply. If I win one soul to the Lord every day, I've added to the Kingdom of God; however, if I win one soul to the Lord every day, and teach them to do the same, I've *multiplied* the Kingdom! God's mandate to men involves more than making converts; it's about making disciples. Dr. Cole said it like this, *"We're building men and raising sons."*

While we should raise our biological children to be mighty men and women of God, this mandate goes beyond our own offspring. How do I know? Simple- Jesus never birthed a son in the natural, and we know He did the will of the Father! **Jesus** fathered men *spiritually.*

Next, we're to fill the earth, which is a natural progression of multiplication. How will we ever subdue the earth unless it's full of God's children? The missing link to this dilemma is a Christ-like man who possesses the very spirit and nature of God!

Everything God does is according to a pattern based on a principle. God's original commission given to Adam in the Garden tells us what we're to do (Genesis 1:28). The Great Commission (**Matthew 28:18-20**) tells us how we're to do it- "**Go and make disciples of all the nations.**" God has laid down the plan in the beginning, and then Jesus showed us the pattern to achieve it.

The truth is, when we hear the word discipleship, most Christians think of a Sunday school class or Bible school course. Even though Jesus' last words to us were *"make disciples,"* we've somehow lost sight of the mechanics of true discipleship. While Sunday morning church service is a vital part of our spiritual growth, that's only a portion of discipleship. Discipleship takes place primarily outside the four walls of the church, in everyday life and by someone willing to invest his time, energy, and prayers into someone else. It is only when we are committed to a lifestyle of discipleship that we experience the essence of manhood, the fulfillment of **fathering**, and the excitement of the Gospel.

I remember watching Dr. Cole get off a plane after a ministry trip. He was in his late 70's and had just finished preaching a world tour. I thought about the multitudes of men Dr. Cole's age that are finishing out their lives in nursing homes. For many of them, their physical sickness and pain is not what hurts the most; they are actually dying from a broken heart and unfulfilled, unrealized dreams. They never discovered their purpose in life. And not knowing why they were born torments them day and night. As the character William Wallace so eloquently said in the movie *Braveheart*, "All men die; few men really ever live." The greatest gift a **father** can give his son is to connect him to his purpose. That's what Dr. Cole did for me and for so many others.

> *The greatest gift a father can give his son is to connect him to his purpose.*

As Dr. Cole's funeral came to a close, I found myself meditating on **John 12:24, "Verily, verily, I say to you, except a grain of wheat fall the ground and die, it abideth alone; but if it dies, it bringeth forth much fruit."** As long as Dr. Cole was alive, we would all look to him to lead the way. Now that he was gone, his sons in the faith would each make a decision. *"Am I going to run with the baton that Dr. Ed Cole worked so hard to put into my hands? Am I willing to do for others what Dr. Cole has done for me?"* If so, Dr. Cole's ministry to men would become exponential and *bring forth much fruit.*

Revelation seemed to flood my spirit that day, and I began

to clearly see what God would have me say at Dr. Cole's home going service. The message he birthed in me stayed with me long after the memorial service and has become my heart's cry to men today. It has become the motivation for this book and the inspiration for my life.

A great deal of this book is about Dr. Cole, but I'm not writing it for him. He has gone on to his heavenly reward, and I'm sure any earthly recognition this book may bring hardly matters to him. Though I will be sharing my personal testimonies and experiences in the upcoming chapters, this book is certainly not about me. The truth is, this book is about you.

DASH

You have been given a dash. What do I mean? Someday, all of us will breath our last breath. The only thing that will separate our birthdate from our final day on earth is a dash. The question will be, *"What did I do with my 'dash': the years, days, and hours God entrusted to me?"* At that point, it will be too late to change the answer.

I remember running the 100 yard dash in high school. It was a fantastic feeling to cross the finish line, look back, and realize that I had successfully completed the race. That is exactly how God wants us to feel about our life when we approach our last lap. **"I have fought the good fight, I have finished my course, I have kept the faith." (2 Timothy 4:7)**

The remainder of this book is designed to connect you with a practical and powerful way to make the most of your "dash". We will expand our understanding of **fathers** in the faith and come to terms with the crucial knowledge of genuine sonship.

I believe you will be changed, challenged, and charged to embrace discipleship (fathering) at a greater level than you ever have before and leaving you more fulfilled as a man than you ever thought possible. After reading this book, you will be empowered to actually fulfill the grand purpose for which you were created.

Now is the time to act as Maximus said in the movie *Gladiator*, "What we do in this life will echo for all of eternity."

God, I really miss Edwin Louis Cole.

2

GENERATIONAL THINKING

"A man's faith can outlive his life."

To understand what a real father is, we need to look at the best model- Dr. Cole himself. Dr. Edwin Louis Cole's son, Paul Cole, wrote this chapter. I was so moved by his story that I felt it belonged at the beginning of the book.

Somehow, it completes the circle that my last memory of touching my Dad is the prickly, scratching feel of his beard as I leaned down to kiss him goodbye. Then he left. It completes our circle of life, because my identity was formed in the closeness of his face to mine as a young boy.

A man's identity is shaped by the breath of his father. Last moments, last words, last communion, last conversation while over fifty years of life spanned our experience together: son and father. Yet these last moments seem to linger now, with a special bittersweet taste, long after his passing. At times I think of our last conversation.

We were talking after having had communion with my sisters and some friends that were at my Dad's house. He was resting on his bed, the constant pain in his back making it hard to get comfortable in any position. We talked about

Mom, about how great life had been, about my daughter's impending wedding- an assortment of meaningful things. Times now were not given to the frivolous, the moments too few, too precious. We began to speak of the ministry to men that had wonderfully consumed the latter years of his life, his place of fulfillment.

We spoke of victories, past and recent, special friends, and the amazing privilege to have known so many great men. I leaned down to kiss his face and we embraced. As I rose up, he held on to my hand and said, *"Are you going to keep it going?"* He wanted to know about the ministry to men. I squeezed his hand and said, *"Dad, what you started is in the hearts of great men around the world; it can't be stopped. It's in my heart and in the heart of your grandsons, and we will never quit. Don't worry, it will be bigger and stronger; it will happen."*

He let go of my hand, leaned back deep into his pillow and simply said, *"Good."* These were the last words with my Dad.

Dad was saved as a young man, and though he strayed through his late teens and early twenties in the Coast Guard, he was marked for the Gospel. Dad always said he was running fast away from God, but that he *"couldn't outrun his mother's prayers."* He accepted the Lord because his mom never quit praying for him. And his mom, Florence Goodrum Cole, was saved because her sister wouldn't quit praying for her.

Her sister was a slight built woman named Ethel Dean. The world would never know of her, but her prayers caused a stir of righteousness that not only saved all her sisters, but it also saved a young man named Ed Cole, and caused a wave of revival among men of the world. July 1991- at the age of 98, a lady in a small and nondescript house in L.A. died. Eighteen relatives attended her funeral. Living alone for over fifty years, many would say that Ethel Dean lived and died without much impact on the world, but it was quite the contrary.

Ethel Dean had three sisters: Mabel, Berta, and Florence. At the age of 24, Ethel had received Jesus Christ as her Lord and Savior. Longing to see her sisters saved, day after day she began to write to them about Jesus. In tear stained letters after letters, she shared the love of her heavenly Father. First one, then another, and finally all three of her sisters accepted Jesus.

One sister, Florence, was so taken by her newfound relationship with God that she immediately enrolled in a Bible college (LIFE Institute in Los Angeles) with Aimee Semple Mcpherson as her teacher. Weekend nights would find Florence in the street corners of L.A. preaching the Gospel with her 12-year-old son reluctantly playing the trombone. That young lad, confused by the drinking of his father and a dysfunctional home life, went through some tough times of indecision, but Florence and her sister Ethel wouldn't let go. They did what they knew to do- they prayed.

On one occasion, in World War II, as the kamikaze attacks came on that young man's ship, Florence was awakened in the night. She prayed, and miraculously the dive-bombers missed his ship. Then, there was the day that Florence found out her son was attending a Sunday night church service. She drove to the city where he lived, parked down the street, got in the back seat, and prayed all afternoon. That night, her son committed his life to the Lord and was called into ministry.

The legacy of that fragile soft-spoken little lady named Ethel Dean is a worldwide Christian Men's Movement. She lived ninety-eight years somewhat anonymously. Her sister Florence's son was named Edwin...

I remember my great aunt Ethel was soft, quiet, and peaceful. She never got any credit, but Dad never forgot Aunt Ethel and her legacy. **His great strength was that he *never forgot those that prayed for him* and those who received no recognition; he was gracious to those the world would never recognize. He took pleasure blessing those who**

never seemed to get a pat on the back. He was there to tell you, *"You did great,"* and was there to tell you where you needed to improve, since he wanted you to be your best.

Dad taught me to create the world I live in on purpose. *"Don't let others create your world for you, they will always create it too small."* He taught me that men must be intimately involved in each others lives, that discipling men is to learn to be vulnerable, and that too many men want to preach sermons behind the pulpit, but that won't change the world. Teaching men truth will change a man's heart, and that will change the world. He taught me to commit to truth and to love the Word.

My life is made up of the things that came out of Dad's heart, the words of his mouth, and the prayers of my mom. I was blessed to know the love of wonderful parents and to feel the warmth of an embrace and smile of a Dad who is proud of his kids.

I can still feel his beard on my face.

3

MATURITY

"Manhood and Christlikeness are synonymous."

D r. Cole always had a way of saying so much with just a few words. I'll never forget the day I first heard him say, *"Manhood and Christlikeness are synonymous."* That simple, yet supernatural statement, forever changed the destiny of my life.

When I first heard of Dr. Cole, I was the principal at a Christian school. I already had my first son, who we named Cole before we ever heard of Dr. Cole. I don't know for sure if that was prophetic or not, but I like to think it was.

At the time, I had a big closet that I, and other staff members, used to store books and tapes in at work. A co-worker and minister by the name of James Benson approached me and said, "You know, there is a good book in that closet by Ed Cole called *Maximized Manhood*. If you haven't read it yet, you should!" Well, that bore witness with my spirit, but unfortunately my flesh didn't care what my spirit had to say.

For two solid years, every time I passed that closet I thought of the book, but I never once ventured in to pick it up and read it. Now, when I come across men with that same complacency, I have compassion and patience because I realize the ignorance we all dwell in until something or someone gives us the motivation to reach for higher and deeper spiritual truth.

Two years after James first mentioned *Maximized Manhood* to me, the topic managed to surface again. We were building an addition to our Christian school at the time, and James and I were in the car together headed downtown to pick up an air conditioning duct. I noticed he had a bucket full of tapes and books in his car, which he told me he planned to disperse the materials during his next ministry visit in the jails. I began rummaging through the merchandise only to find I had pulled out a tape by Dr. Cole. I said to James, *"Hey, isn't this the same guy who wrote that book that you told me about awhile back?"* We put the tape in and began to listen.

Mediocre men want authority without accountability.

One of the first statements that Dr Cole made during the message was, *"Mediocre men want authority without accountability."* The profound truth hit me like a train! At that time in my life, I was struggling through issues with other staff members and men, and this revelation brought a newfound clarity to my situation. I was so impressed with the **relevance** and **practicality** of that statement that I hungered for more (like I recently hungered for a Whataburger after returning home from Europe)! Ed Cole went on to say that, *"Manhood and Christlikeness are synonymous."* He explained that the closest we ever come to being a real man is to be like Christ, because there is no better definition of a man than one who is willing to give his life for a higher cause. As I listened, I couldn't help but wonder where this man had been all my life.

As the tape continued to play, the truth I heard literally shook my soul. I began to repent, because I had put off reading this man's book. **I was two years behind!**

DR. COLE'S DEFINITION OF MATURITY

I'll never forget hearing Dr. Cole's definition of maturity for the first time. *"Maturity does not come with age, but with the acceptance of responsibility."* Dr. Cole taught that physical maturation is the natural result of time, but spiritual and emotional maturity does not "just happen." It is only when we are willing to take responsibility for our actions that we can be called mature. Just like physical maturity transforms a boy into a man, spiritual maturity separates the men from the boys.

Christ is the ultimate example of a man, because he was the ultimate example of maturity. While most of us struggle just to take responsibility for our own actions, Jesus took it a step further and took responsibility for others actions! It wasn't His sin that put Him on the cross- it was yours and mine. He not only died for the sins of the past, but for sins that were yet to be committed as well. He took responsibility for the transgressions that had happened, were happening, and would happen.

> *Christ is the ultimate example of a man because He is the ultimate example of maturity.*

An immature person is selfish, while a mature person chooses to be selfless. Jesus paid a debt he did not owe and paid a price we could not afford. *Mediocre men want authority without accountability,* but Jesus said that through His accountability He will gain authority. He is the most mature being that has ever walked this earth, which is why *"Manhood and Christlikeness are synonymous."*

NATURE'S ILLUSTRATION

Immaturity is the natural result of fatherlessness. Even nature illustrates this principle. In the plains of South

Africa some years ago, a group of wildlife conservationists sought to relocate a safari habitat to a larger, more ideal location. There was a great expense associated with transporting the animals, and the larger the animal, the greater the cost. As a result, they moved the younger, smaller animals within each species first, and left the older animals to be moved at a later time.

Poaching is a constant problem in Africa, so when the conservationist discovered that all of their young male white rhinos at the new habitat were dead, they assumed that's what had happened. However, upon closer examination, there were no bullet wounds or indications that poachers were responsible. Further investigations led them to a shocking discovery. The young male elephants had become so territorial that they killed all the male rhinos. They also impregnated the young female elephants prematurely.

The conservationist had no choice but to spend the necessary money and transport the larger, older, and more mature bull male elephants to the reserve. They hoped that their presence would alleviate the unruly behavior of the younger males – and they were right! All violent behavior and aggression towards the females immediately stopped.

Without a father's example, discipline, and supervision, young men do not mature.

For every effect there is a cause. The reason so many American men live in rebellion, promiscuity, and poor judgment is because there are not enough **fathers** in the land. We are lacking the "big bull elephants" called fathers. Without a father's example, discipline, and supervision, young men do not mature; however, when fathers have a presence in their home, church, and community, **order is restored.**

THE BOOK THAT CHANGED MY LIFE

The first thing I did upon returning to the church after listening to Dr. Cole's tapes was dig *Maximized Manhood* out of the closet, dusted it off, and consumed the wisdom found on every page. It took me one day to read the entire book, and I read it again the next day. I circled, underlined, and highlighted as I picked each sentence apart; I must have read through that book no less than 50 times. Dr. Cole's profound one-liners, often referred to as "Coleisms" , immediately became a natural part of my everyday vocabulary (this is a recommendation for you!)

A few months later, Allen Martin asked me to share a word with some inmates during a ministry trip to the Galveston County Jail. The short notice left me no time to prepare a message, so I just grabbed my Bible and my worn copy of *Maximized Manhood* and accepted the invitation to speak. All I knew to do was open up Dr. Cole's book and read the words that had so drastically impacted my own life.

As I began sharing out of the third chapter entitled, **"The Playboy Problem,"** the inmates actually stood up, jumped, and shouted! Using Dr. Cole's book made it easy to break down the simple truth that what we call "problems," God calls sins. As long as we classify our sins as problems, we seek only treatments to pacify our behavior. Once we call it what it is – sin – we have to confront it and get rid of it!

> *What we call "problems," God calls sin.*

Prisoners, men of large stature and rugged in appearance, wept and mourned over their sins. As I looked around the room I saw the tremendous potential locked up in that prison – and in those men! They were truly touched, and seeing their sincere transformation brought an inner satisfaction to my life that I'd never tapped into before. I left the Galveston

County Jail that day more convinced than ever that there was something different about this book and something extraordinary about its author, Dr. Cole.

Eventually, I taught *Maximized Manhood* to the students in our adult Bible school as well as the young people in our Christian school. We even found a way to get "Coleisms" into the public school system. We invited athletes and the student bodies from La Marque High School and Galveston Ball High School to breakfast on the morning of game day. They ate up Dr. Cole's truths as much as they did the pancakes! We had between 200 and 300 students who attended weekly from September through November.

MEETING THE MAN

The more I taught out of Dr. Cole's books, the more I felt an inner tugging rising up in me. I wasn't exactly sure what to make of all that I was feeling, but I figured the best place to turn for Godly advice was to the man whose books had changed my life – Dr. Ed Cole. When I realized he lived in Dallas, Texas, just a few hours from me, I wrote him a letter. A world renowned speaker and author of his stature was bound to be extremely busy and might not even read his own mail, but I figured if it was God's plan for me to hear from this man, I would. I sealed the envelope, stuck on a stamp, and prayerfully dropped the letter in the mailbox.

You can image my surprise when, one week later, my secretary walked into my office and said, "*Dr. Edwin Louis Cole is holding for you on line one.*" To this day, she and I both remember that moment clearly, because it was such a shock! It was an honor to have a phone conversation with him, but I felt like I needed more than that. I was confident that he could answer the questions I had circulating in my spirit if only I could have a moment of his time in person. I knew God was calling me into a greater depth of ministry, and I was leaning towards men's ministry in particular. I wanted confirmation and direction. Since I identified with his book so much, I was sure Dr. Cole could provide that. He answered my request for a meeting with a simple "yes" and told me he had about an hour of free time around noon the following day. I told him I would be there!

I headed out the following morning in my Toyota pickup, only to find that the air conditioning quit working within miles from my house. Dallas was 4 hours away and I was going to be a sweaty mess by the time I arrived. I stopped and called my wife and we both agreed that I needed to catch a flight at Hobby airport. I was determined to make it to this meeting, no matter the cost or energy it required. I was convinced God ordained it and that I was going to get the spiritual direction I needed. I later found out that Dr. Cole had just returned from Russia and was leaving for Africa in two days, so this was an extraordinary opportunity to see him.

I arrived in Dallas, rented a car, and drove to the hotel where he was staying. I went to the top floor and thought I had heard his voice (it sounded like his tapes anyway). When the door opened, he was wearing a big black hat, which I later learned that he affectionately called "Akubra." He had on a blue jacket with a blue and yellow tie. The image of my first glimpse of Dr. Cole will permanently stick in my mind. I managed to pick up an instant camera at a gas station on my way up, and we took a picture together. That photo now hangs in my office as a daily reminder of the word I was soon to receive (it is also on the back cover of this book).

We spent the next two hours talking about life, vision, manhood, and fathering. His books say the greatest counselors are the best listeners and that you can answer any man's challenge if you will listen to him long enough. That is exactly what he did. He said, "Ok G.F., you have one hour to just spill your guts and tell me what's on your heart. Tell me about your job, your church, your wife, if you have one,

41

childhood, and everything you can think of."

After I spoke about all of those things in detail, he asked me one more question. *"What is it you desire to do with your life G.F.?"* I responded without hesitation *"I basically want your job, or one just like it. At this point in my life, I would like nothing more than to travel around the world and minster to men. I have been a coach and taught men all my life, so it just seems like all I want to do is minister truths from your books."* He paused a minute and said the words I will never forget:

> G.F., I have met a lot of men in my life, but I see something in you that I haven't seen very often. I see the potential to be a great pastor, one of the greatest I have ever known. You are a leader, an organizer, a motivator, and a strategist, all of which make a great Pastor. However, you are too young, your family is too young, and you have no experience or contacts to do what I do. It would ruin your family life. What I see for you, if that is what you are asking me, is that you should go start your church and *build it on the strength of men. You will have consistency for your wife and children and an outlet to minister to men. If you do this, you will be very successful and build a huge church.*

What fatherly advice and leadership! That was all I needed to hear: that I could do it! I knew God was doing something, but I didn't know it involved pastoring. However, I had already settled in my heart that whatever God, through Dr. Cole, said, even if it was to go home and keep serving in the capacity that it was already in, I was going to do it.

This thought process, giving an elder in the faith liberty

to confirm the will of God in my life, eventually became a foundational principle of our ministry. I knew Dr. Cole was not God, but I respected him as a vehicle through whom God could speak to me. It would have been ignorant for me to pray to God for direction, to have a man of God like Dr. Cole speak into my life, and then ignore what he had to say! Unfortunately, as a pastor, I see that happen all too often today.

Many times, we know deep down what our answer is before we seek advice, but it is not necessarily what we want to hear. Maybe it requires change on our part or more energy than we want to expect, so we place blame on the man who gave the advice instead of heeding his counsel. Better yet, we continue to seek counsel elsewhere until someone tells us what we want to hear even though it is not the will of God for our life.

My meeting with Dr. Cole was a quest for truth and I was committed to follow through with whatever answers I was given. Dr. Cole told me I must do what God has called me to do all while honoring my pastor. *"If God is stirring your spirit to Pastor, you must do it."* He told me to go to Katy, TX, the city God had placed on my heart, start PowerHouse Church, and motivate men to be Godly husbands, fathers and champions.

So, with that simple yet sound word, my family began knocking on doors every Saturday and inviting one family at a time to join the vision. It was a 2-hour trip there and back, but we did it every weekend faithfully. We told people about our supernatural church before there were ever people in it! We started the church in faith, applying principles my pastor, Walter Hallam, had instilled in me. His guidance and example were of great value, and more than ever, I appreciated his friendship and shepherding. After all, he was the one that helped save my marriage long before I had ever heard of Dr. Cole.

We held our first service on Sunday, June 16, 1996.

It was Father's Day. We were believing for 100 people to attend, but we did not give into discouragement when 10 people actually came.

One year later, our congregation had grown to 200. Dr. Cole and Pastor Hallam both attended our one-year anniversary dedication service. Dr. Cole came back several other times and spoke. He became so much more than an eloquent speaker and spiritual icon in my life. He took on the role of a mentor, spiritual coach, and father. It was during this time that I came to understand the role of spiritual father and embrace the benefits of such a relationship.

FATHERS IN THE FAITH

When I initially contacted Dr. Cole, I was not attempting to become his spiritual son. To be quite honest, I didn't know much about spiritual sonship, because it is not something that we see modeled in the local church. The few examples I had seen left a bad impression on me. All I saw were "fathers" who demanded a great deal from their sons in the faith and gave little or no support in return.

The Bible clearly shows us that a father initiates relationship with his son. Consider Abraham and Issac, the story of the prodigal son, and even God with Jesus. Fathers invest in their sons and as a result, their sons give back to them. Dr. Cole called me even when I hadn't taken the time to call him.

A father initiates relationship with his son.

He willingly ministered at my church without making a single reference to collecting an honorarium. He took the initiative to call my wife and maintain a relationship with her. He spent time discussing the more personal issues in my life with me. We never signed a contract that declared a father-son relationship between us, but it just happened naturally as a result of

44

Dr. Cole's care for me. All my misconceptions about spiritual fathers were no longer a concern. I had found the real thing.

We can't "throw the baby out with the bathwater." If you have heard, seen, or even experienced negative situations involving fathers in the faith, don't give up. There are genuine fathers out there, and we all need one!

Many churches are structured like a corporation-everyone knows their place on the leadership ladder and pretty much sticks to their "rung" until there is a vacancy that requires promoting. Relationships within the Church Body are genuine, yet lacking in intimacy. We attempt to quench our desire to grow spiritually by listening to our pastors sermons, watching how he treated his family at the church picnic, and hanging on to his every word during a marriage counseling session.

I think every Christian who truly strives for spiritual maturity comes to a place in life where we ask, "What does everyday Christianity look like?" We want to be taught and led to see the invisible so we can do the seemly impossible. We have questions, but we are not sure whom to ask. We're entangled in a certain sin, but we don't know whom we can confide in without being judged. We feel confused, but

There are genuine fathers out there and we all need one!

we are not sure who to call for direction. **"We have ten thousand instructors, but we have not many fathers" (1 Corinthian 4:15a).**

I am so glad Dr. Cole not only understood that scripture, but fulfilled it in my life. As verse 16 goes on to say, **"Therefore, I urge you to imitate me [the apostle Paul]."** Dr. Cole followed Paul's example and, **"Became my father in the Gospel in Christ Jesus" (1 Corinthians 4:15b).** He came out from behind the pulpit and let me see the person he

was in everyday settings, dealing with everyday situations. It was like reading a "pop-up" book version of the Bible. I not only read what the scripture said, I saw the practical application in the life of Edwin Louis Cole. It was an invaluable experience that transformed my marriage, launched our ministry, and led me to much deeper and greater level of relationship with God. He built my house!

FINDING THE SPIRITUAL FATHER

As you read about my relationship with Dr. Cole, you may find yourself wondering, "Where's my Dr. Cole? How do I find a spiritual father?" Here are a few steps you can take to identify the man who is to become such an intricate part of your life.

One – Pray! We need the Spirit of God to lead us in the right direction and orchestrate the relationship. While there are certain criteria we should look for in a spiritual father, we cannot rely solely on our own reasoning. We need God to confirm our decision. If God's not in it, we have no business pursuing it; no matter how "right" it may seem to us.

I want to point out that it was God who opened up the doors of opportunity for me to meet a man of Dr. Cole's stature. Please do not get caught up in the idea that you must serve under a "famous" man of God. You don't want to show up on the doorstep of your favorite TV evangelist, whom you've never met, and ask him to be your Father! Your mentor is most likely going to be an ordinary man who possesses a supernatural spiritual walk. He may not have his name flashing in lights at conventions centers all over the country, but if he is a man of integrity and faith, he is worthy of your allegiance and submission "as unto the Lord."

Two – Identify your **purpose.** Chances are your spiritual Father will be a man with similar vision and purpose. Zero in on where your passion lies and look for a man who shares a common focus. You want someone who is traveling the path that you see yourself on, except who is farther along. His experience will then be relevant and applicable to you.

Zero in on where your passion lies and look for a man who shares a common focus.

Three- Evaluate his track record. Does he currently disciple men on a consistent basis? Does he relate to men of various levels of leadership, or does he tend to disregard those who have not risen to his degree of leadership? No matter what ministerial accomplishments he may have achieved, if he does not possess a father's heart, he is not the one. Remember, just because a man has a dynamic speaking gift, does not mean he will make a good spiritual father. A mans' spiritual gifts are not indicative of his ability or willingness to disciple.

Once you feel like you've identified a prospect, do not expect him to throw his arms around you and call you son! **Relationships take time to develop**. I suggest that you buy his tapes, read his books, attend his ministry functions, and become a servant. Chances are, he's seen many people come and go, **but your faithfulness** will be an indication that you are sincere and trustworthy.

This isn't about forcing your way into his life. While you express your desire for a deeper relationship with him, you cannot demand that he reciprocate the same level of commitment immediately. God will be the one to eventually draw his attention to you and open the doors to greater levels of discipleship. In the meantime, learn what you can from the information made available to you.

I believe Dr. Cole reached out to me because he recognized how much I valued his messages and ministry. I diligently listened to all of his tapes and read all of his books. His words became second nature to me, and every message I preached included his "Coleisms." We don't have to wait until we're in the presence of our spiritual father before we can learn from him. We should avail ourselves to all of his ministry tools and seek to learn that way as well. Then, when we do have the opportunity to spend time with him, our conversations are magnified.

In our day of podcasts and iPhones, we can allow many voices to impact our lives. Don't be deceived that there are many teachers, but not necessarily fathers. A good rule of thumb is that a one-way teaching can be a seed spreading session, but that doesn't lead to accountability. A father not only teaches, but he also is responsible for the daily guiding, guarding, and governing of the son. As it is in the natural, so it is in the spiritual- our society has a lot of "bumblebee" preachers that float from flower to flower pollinating. What we really need is an influx of responsible fathers that daily disciple the new babies until they mature into men of God.

It may take some time to find your spiritual father, but stick to it! When you do find him, cherish that relationship and honor him with your time, talent, and treasure.

God, I sure do miss Dr. Cole!

4

MAKING OF A CHAMPION

~~~

"Champions are made, not born."

This chapter was written by Dr. Cole and was taken out of his book, *Absolute Answers* (published by Thomas Nelson, distributed by C. M. N.). It gives us a glimpse into Dr. Cole's rocky relationship with his own father and how he beat the odds to become "The father of the Christian Men's Movement."

I followed my dad's pattern but could not outrun my mother's prayers. I imitated my dad's lifestyle, which put me on a road to devastation, but I became an answer to my mother's prayers.

It seems awkward to start about talking about things as personal as my relationship with my father, but that relationship illustrates what this book is all about. I was a prodigal. I wandered far from God and the faith of my mother. But, as you can see, the story of the prodigal is the story of all humanity – though not all return to the father.

Dad's lifestyle was a road to self-destruction; moms pathway led to a long, good life, riches, honor, pleasure, and peace **(Proverbs 3:15-18).**

My dad was quite the quintessential, "hail-fellow-well-met." He never met a stranger. Conviviality was his forte, personal pleasure his love, and work his passion.

He was a mathematical genius in my eyes. He could add a column of five digit figures almost as swiftly as a calculator. He worked in later life in the State and then the federal revenue departments, and he was always given their most difficult cases. Seldom, if ever, could bookkeepers and accountants hide anything from him. But he was so ingratiating, it took the sting out of the fine if they had to come up with more money.

When he died, more than 300 men attended his funeral, crowding the chapel. Most of the people from both offices where he had worked were there. So was the bookie with whom him he placed his bets on horse races, the news vendor from the corner where he worked, two waitresses from the restaurant where he ate lunch, as well as many others the family I had never met.

He was listed in the telephone directory as E. L. "King" Cole, the only person at the time listed by his nickname in the Los Angeles phonebook, because he was known simply as "King". At times, when I was a young boy and he introduced me to people, Dad would say, "he's just the clown Prince." Everyone would laugh at me.

Dad loved sports and would bet on all of them. Mom never knew how much money he really made until he died. When the report came for estate tax purposes, she was amazed at the amount that had been spent on sports or lost on betting.

I heard the attack on Pearl Harbor announced at a professional football game Dad and I were attending at Gilmore Stadium in Los Angeles. It was only one of the many sports venues we visited, and after he died, I continued to love the sports he taught me. He lived for pleasure of every kind, including alcohol.

We had a troubled household when dad was drinking, and in time I became resentful of it. At times when alcohol was unkind to him, he was unkind to others. Oddly, rather than it driving me to a hatred of alcohol, it did just the opposite. It produced a determination in me to "show him," not by never tasting alcohol, but by developing an ability to do it more and better than he did. One night after receiving a whipping from him that I felt was unfair, I crawled into bed and tearfully vowed that I would out drink him. That resolution was almost my undoing.

Mom became a Christian years earlier, shortly after they married in Texas. Her sister Ethel had been converted in Los Angeles and wrote most glowing, intimate, precious letters to my mother of her experience and love for the Lord. Aunt Ethel cried when she wrote one of them, and her tears stained the pages. Those tear stains were partly responsible for mother attending a tent meeting in Dallas where she, too, was converted.

Not long after that, mom packed me up, a four-year-old at the time, and we traveled to Los Angeles where she attended a Bible school with her sisters, Ethel and Berta. Dad didn't go with us. It wasn't what he wanted, but mom went anyway. Since he loved us and mom wouldn't budge, he eventually joined us.

I missed much of the good part of my high school years due to my preoccupation with learning to drink like that. Immediately after graduation, when war broke out, some friends and I enlisted in the United States Coast Guard. Waiting for induction after enlisting, I went to work at the new Marine base they were building at Camp Pendleton in Southern California. My father was the Navy's timekeeper for all personnel on the base.

One evening, Dad invited me to go with him to his friend's house where some fellows were getting together. It was just a group of men from work, a "guy thing," spending an evening talking and drinking. There was nothing out of the ordinary in that, but it became an extraordinary night for me.

Late that evening, I crossed through the living room of the home we were in, holding a glass full of whiskey and drinking it straight, when I walked by the couch where my Dad was passed out from drinking. I looked at him at that moment and thought, *I won; I out-drank him!* It was a moment of triumph, one I had looked forward to for so long.

Yet, when I continued out the door into the field in front of the house, I looked up into the starry sky and, instead of gloating, I cried, *"Is this all there is?"* Having reached my goal, such as it was, I felt lonely, desolate, empty, and lost. It was one of the saddest moments of my life.

No exultation of victory; only a dead, dry defeat. I was like the prodigal sitting among the pigs in the far country. As I sat down on the old porch chair, I let out a groan – mourning for what had been taken from me by pursuing a dream that it proved to be so worthless. I spent some time that night trying to resolve the disappointment and the issues it raised.

Finally, I came to a firm conviction: mom was right; dad was wrong. Like the prodigal in the parable, I was finally "coming to myself" and realizing the truth.

Not until after the war years, however, would I accept and apply that truth personally. My life then would radically change through Christ's saving grace. My mother's prayers prevailed against my dad's pattern.

God answers prayer!

Mom would live to see me enter the ministry, help support me and my family in those early years, grow to love my wife as her own daughter, and take personal joy in every step of growth God brought us. But that night, years before, one dream died, and I went years without another to replace it until the Lord put a new dream in my heart. The new dream, birthed by God's Spirit, was to tell everyone I could of the great gift of salvation God gives through Christ.

After a few years in the military, having married while in uniform, I returned home and went to work for a great Christian man, Ralph Calkins, who was like a second father to me. On the job, it was an ever-new delight to tell someone of a fresh truth I had learned from Scripture, exhort him to read the Bible, and find for himself the most exciting life on earth. Some did. Some didn't.

Because we were near the Marine base where I'd worked before, off-duty Marines would wander around town. I eagerly met them, invited them to a "hospitality home" through our church, had them fed with a good, home-cooked meal, and then told them of God's great love for them.

In those early years, I also went back to preach on the street corner in Los Angeles where mom had taken me as a boy. She and others would sing, play their instruments, testify, preach, and pray with men who were living on skid row.

(Author's Note: To realize an effective and impactful ministry, a man must be willing to obtain as well as maintain. In other words, he must evangelize as well as pastor (father). It's been my experience that most men do one or the other, rarely both, and then wonder why their ministry remains small. Remember that Jesus is the alpha and omega not the alpha or omega. If you aren't willing to do both, don't start a ministry; simply remain under someone who is already successful in both.

Take this story as an example. A hot dog vendor in New York City begins his business by renting a stand. He is unashamed of his product so he shouts out to everyone, "Hotdogs! Get your hotdogs here!" He simultaneously cooks the hotdogs for the potential customers. He greets the customer, relates to them, asks them what they would like on their hotdogs, introduces them to new mustard or other toppings, and encourages them to come back and bring their friends and family. He also educates his customer as to when and where he will be serving great hotdogs in the future. Oh yes, he also keeps the area around him clean so that can create an atmosphere that fosters trust from the future customer. I'm so glad my mentor, Ed Cole, began preaching on the street. Much like this hot dog vendor, a minister is an entrepreneur of eternal significance.)

My new dream was to share the good news not only with such men, but also with my Dad. And I did. I longed to see him love the Lord and for us to be united as a family in faith. I started traveling to see him as often as I could, telling him what God was doing in my life, explaining what a wonderful Savior Jesus was, and how satisfied in the field I was now. For four months I carried out this plan.

I wasn't there when it happened, but mom called and told me when dad made his commitment to Christ. What a thrill! Then, just four days later, Dad collapsed in mom's arms from an unsuspected blood clot that had reached his heart. He was gone, suddenly, before I had a chance to see him one last time. But it was done; the dream had been realized.

In the almost 50 years since, I've seen hard times, good times, easy times, and tense times. But all of those years have been spent serving the Lord. Then came the day in 1995 when I had the opportunity to realize yet another part of the dream God had given me. I was invited to be a guest minister at a Promise Keepers meeting at the Los Angeles Coliseum.

The Coliseum isn't far from the home where I grew up, from the places where I had spent my childhood and adolescence, and from Belmont High School where I graduated. Standing on a huge platform at one end of the Coliseum, I looked at what was announced to be the largest gathering of Christian men in the world up to that moment. It had been filled when I was there previously with Dad for various events, but never with men only, and especially with men who were followers of Christ.

After finishing my teaching, I exercised a moment of pulpit privilege. Boldly, I declared my intention:

> Gentlemen, you are seated in a stadium and on a field where I've watched the great Jackie Robinson, Kenny Washington, and Woodrow Strode play football for the University of California at Los Angeles. I watched Cotton Warburton, Doyle Nave, and "Antelope" Al Krueger play football for the University of Southern California. I came here for the Olympic Games with my parents in 1932 and attended them again with my wife in 1984. When the Dodgers moved here from New York, I watched them play their first baseball game in this place. I took my wife out on our first date here to watch a football game with me. And all of that time, I have seen some great plays and heard some great cheering, but I've never heard this stadium full of men give the greatest cheer possible. In a moment, I'm going to ask you to stand. When I count to three, I want you to give the loudest cheer and shout ever heard in this place. We will do it for the Winner of winners, the Champion of all champions – our Lord Jesus Christ!

I counted; they shouted. It was, without a doubt, the greatest and loudest shout ever heard of that place.

Dreams do come true. Only God can take a lonely empty, lost young man standing in a field in the middle of nowhere and years later put him on the stage in front of more than 72,000 men to lead a shout to the glory of God.

As I write this now, I think of my dad. But it's at my

mother's graveside that I stop and thank her for what she meant to my life.

Dad's pattern could not prevail against mom's prayers. This prodigal came all the way home in more ways than one.

5

GOD'S FINAL PLAN

~~~

**"While man looks for better methods, God looks
for better men."**

My wife, Rose, and I like to get away periodically and
just spend some quality time together. One weekend
in particular, we were getting ready to go eat at a nice restaurant on the Riverwalk in San Antonio, Texas. The restaurant was just a few blocks away from our hotel and since
it was beautiful outside, I thought it would be nice to walk
there. What I didn't know was that my wife's new shoes
were already hurting her feet before we even left our room.
When I suggested that we walk, she resisted the urge to
demand that we drive. Instead, she just put a smile on her
face and counted down the blocks as we made our way to
the restaurant.

While we enjoyed our delicious meal, Rose was silently
dreading the walk back. As we left the table and headed for
the door, her decision to lovingly submit now seemed like a
huge mistake. Right as she was wondering if her feet could
possibly take another step, an elegant horse and carriage
pulled up in front of us. She didn't know that I had arranged
for a romantic ride around the city.

We had a wonderful time that night. As the carriage

stopped in front of our hotel, Rose couldn't help but marvel to herself. If she had complained about walking and insisted that we take the car, it would have ruined the surprise and spoiled our date.

Human beings have struggled with the word submit since the beginning of time. Submission goes against everything our flesh stands for. Human nature always seems to want to do things our way, in our time, and on our terms. This tendency is something we must confront in our own lives if we're ever going to become the spiritual sons that God wants us to be.

The truth is, you cannot have submission until you first have disagreement. For example, it's easy to submit when we agree with all the procedures and protocols our supervisor asks of us, but what happens when we're asked to do something we'd rather not do? If we're suddenly expected to clock in at 6:00am instead of the usual 8:00am, our ability to submit will be tested! Furthermore, if I manage to get myself to work in time to clock in at 6:00am, but I'm complaining and murmuring against my boss the entire time, I'm still not submitting.

You cannot have submission until you first have disagreement.

True submission begins in the heart. We make a commitment to yield to the leadership of another and we respond to their instructions with joy, even when it's not what we want. It actually takes a much stronger person to submit than it does to rebel. Anyone can throw their hands up and tell their boss, *"You're wrong and I'm not doing it."* However, it takes faith and character to say, *"I don't agree with this new procedure, but I'm going to do it anyway. God will make sure I'm taken care of in the end."* Of course, we never submit to sin or do anything that violates God's Word. Other than that, we're to obey those God placed in authority over us.

TWO KINDS OF AUTHORITY

"Everyone must submit himself to the governing authorities, for there is no authority except that which God has established. The authorities that exist have been established by God. Consequently, anyone who rebels against the authority is rebelling against what God has instituted and those who do so will bring judgment on themselves" (Romans 13:1-2).

There are two kinds of authority- *natural and spiritual.* In the natural, we have laws established by the government and enforced by police officers. When we see the badge, we know we're dealing with authority. Likewise, there is such thing as spiritual authority. God has established His laws and He uses men and women of God to enforce them.

God calls His children to various degrees of authority within the Body of Christ, and we're to respect our spiritual leaders. **Hebrew 13:17** says, **"Obey your leaders and submit to their authority. They keep watch over you as men who must give an account. Obey them so that their work will be a joy, not a burden, for that would be of no advantage to you."**

If we're ever going to enjoy the benefits of spiritual son-ship, we're going to have to learn to submit. Knowledge comes from reading the Bible, but *understanding* comes from *standing under* a spiritually mature believer. As we observe their lifestyle of faith and embrace their spiritual coaching, we start to understand spiritual truths at an accelerated rate. However, if we resent their authority and constantly rebel against their counsel, we will never gain a lick of understanding. **Proverbs 19:27** warns us, **"Stop listening to instructions, my son, and you will stray from the words of knowledge."**

Understanding comes from "standing under" a spiritually mature believer.

59

I have found myself teaching this principle frequently, so I would like to take the time to comment on the pathway of "Divine intelligence". It comes in 3 steps: knowledge, wisdom, and understanding. We get knowledge from reading or hearing a lecture. It is the acquiring of facts. Second is understanding, which comes by assimilating the facts we acquired in the first step. Understanding happens by standing under another's guidance, tutelage, coaching, and example by submitting to them. You should also remember that this step is a critical door to the final stage, wisdom. The Proverbs tell us that Wisdom is the principle thing - "With all your getting, get wisdom" (Proverbs 4:6). "The fear of the Lord is the beginning of wisdom" (Proverbs 9:10). **Wisdom is the correct usage of the facts acquired and assimilated.**

A man who acquires certain science facts has the knowledge to build a nuclear energy plant. If he uses the understanding correctly, he could supply energy to millions of people, but if he uses it incorrectly, he could build a nuclear bomb and bring devastation to the plant. Knowledge→ understanding (submission) → wisdom.

Dr. Cole always said, *"Obedience is God's method of protection for our life."* I saw that revelation literally play out before my very eyes during a ministry trip to Port Harcourt, Nigeria.

My wife, Rose, and my son, Cole, were overseas with me where the environment was very chaotic and political unrest made the overpopulated dirt roads a dangerous place to be. I was in a car with a local pastor and Rose was riding with his wife in the car behind us. Vehicles seemed to head in every direction, and the never-ending road construction confused all traffic laws. In the middle of this unnerving experience, our situation took a turn for the worse, literally! We were approaching a major traffic jam when our driver suddenly took our car over a median and began driving the other way into incoming traffic. I watched in horror in the rearview mirror as my wife's vehicle approached the median to follow us, only to be stopped by two military officers holding AK-47 rifles. The soldiers instructed the ladies that they were not to cross the median, but the pastor's wife firmly instructed their driver to proceed. The armed men began threatening to shoot out their tires, but the woman relentlessly insisted that they make the turn and follow her husband.

> *Obedience is God's method of protection for our life.*

Our car suddenly stopped, and the pastor got out and began shouting at the soldiers. Much to our relief, this pastor was a well-known man in the city and the hostile men immediately recognized him and honored his request. I remember thinking that he looked like an angel in his long flowing African garb. The soldiers apologized for the way they treated his wife and permitted their car to pass.

While Rose was picking her heart up off the floorboard, she heard the persistent pastor's wife say something she will never forget: *"I knew if my husband got me into this mess, he's going to have to get me out!"* She was willing to follow her husband knowing that God would have to give him the ability to rescue her. That man was her spiritual head and it was God who gave him to her **(Ephesians 5:23).** If God gave him the thought to lead her that way, He would equip him to bring her through safely. She put her trust into God's system by submitting to her husband. That is the way we must all relate to spiritual authority. God puts people in authority, so He is ultimately in charge.

Just like that woman picked that particular man to be her husband and spiritual covering, we are free to pick our spiritual father as well. When we've identified the man we want to follow after, we must follow through with our end of the commitment by trusting in God's ability to work through him.

Dr. Cole taught me that submission is not something we demand; it is something we earn as we model a submitted life. It's much easier to pull a string than to push it, and it's much easier to lead by example than to press people in a direction they don't want to go. When submission is forced, it requires violence and brutality. Submission is intended to be a gift given to the person who will someday give account for our soul.

Men, our wives are asked to submit to us. That means we will someday look God in the face and give account for our stewardship over them. Pastors, elders, leaders, and everyone who is given spiritual authority will give account for those God entrusts to our care in this life. Which is easier, submitting to someone or giving account to God for someone else's life?

AN IMPOSSIBLE STATEMENT

Occasionally, Christians will make comments like, *"I don't need to submit to a person. I submit to God and He's all I need!"* This is actually an impossible statement.

By not submitting to man, we're not submitting to God! **Ephesians 5:21** tells us to **"submit to one another out of reverence for Christ."** God established submission and we are disrespecting Christ when we refuse to submit.

No one, not even God, lives free of submission. Children submit to their parents, wives submit to their husbands, and husbands submit to Christ. The Holy Ghost speaks only what He hears from Jesus. Jesus is submitted to Father God. God is submitted to His word! If the trinity submits, shouldn't we? It's God's pattern for victory for His people.

Submission makes mentoring and discipleship possible.

Submission makes mentoring and discipleship possible. Submitting to Dr. Cole gave him the liberty to tell me the truth in instances when I need to hear it. He knew that I was willing to let him "cut on my flesh" if that's what it took to mend my spirit. **Proverbs 13:1** says, **"A wise son heeds his father's instruction, but a mocker does not listen to his rebuke."**

John Eldredge makes a great point in his book, Wild at Heart. He says that even though we, as men, need father figures to speak sobering truths into our lives, we often pursue more of a "mother figure,"- someone who kisses our "boo-boo's" and allows us to remain little boys. **God will send men into our lives to grow us up,** but if we're not careful, our pride will put a clamp on God's spiritual conduit.

We have to be careful that we do not become so spiritual that we're of no earthly good. Dr. Cole often said, *"A man is only qualified to lead to the degree he is willing to serve."* Consequently, when we consider ourselves too "spiritual" to submit to the discipleship of another man, we can never be used to disciple others, thus becoming "no earthly good."

GOD HAS ALWAYS USED ONE PERSON

What would Elisha have been without Elijah, Moses without Jethro, Esther without Mordeacai, Timothy without Paul, or Joseph without Jacob? The Bible contains more than 32 examples of men and women who submitted to the spiritual leadership of a mentor.

God is not nearly as concerned with what He needs to do as He is with whom He can get to do it! That's why Dr. Cole said, *"While man looks for better methods, God looks for better men."* God didn't send an angel to lead the children of Israel out of bondage, He sent Moses. God didn't use heavenly beings to defeat Goliath. He used David. God hasn't commanded angels to preach the Gospel; He's commanded you and me.

God is not nearly as concerned with what He needs to do, as He is with whom He can get to do it!

God even used people to write the Bible. Each word came from the heart and mind of God (**2 Timothy 3:16**), but He gave man the task of writing it down. Furthermore, God is so determined to use mankind to build His Kingdom, He made His own Son a man! **"The Word became flesh and dwelt among us" (John 1:14).** The victory that changed the destiny of mankind for all eternity was only possible through the vehicle of human flesh.

Father/son relationships within the Body of Christ are not about control, manipulation, or personal power. They are about support, guidance, and discipleship. I have often told the men I mentor that they do not need my permission; they need my advice. I want to see them win and succeed, so I use the Word and the experience I've gained over the years to help direct, not dictate their lives. Dr. Cole taught me, *"It is not the father's responsibility to make children's decisions for them, but to let them see him make his."*

As a Pastor, I am called to be a covering, not a lid. A lid is someone who always worries about the people under him bubbling up over him or becoming greater than himself. A covering is like the basket baby Moses traveled in. We offer protection and support to people while allowing them to go where God is taking them, even if it moves them out of the home.

If we approach submission with fear and we're afraid of being hurt or taken advantage of, we will miss out on God's age-old method of spiritual growth and promotion. Unfortunately, there have been "movements" in the past that were anything but spiritual that have caused many to become suspicious of mentoring relationships within the church. Some years ago, in the name of "discipleship," an organization of people were taken advantage of and mistreated, leaving them hurt and confused. It was unfortunate, but not unpredictable. The devil has always taken God's most effective strategies and perverted them to deceive people and harden their hearts toward the truth.

The father/son relationships I am encouraging do not involve destruction and deception. I simply want to model the example Jesus set for us. We can't allow someone's bad decisions to stop us from using God's perfect patterns!

Dr. Cole was instrumental in my spiritual walk, but it was God who gets the ultimate glory for the victories I've had in my life. I loved Dr. Cole, the man, but it was the Spirit of God inside of Dr. Cole that brought the miraculous into my life.

Dr. Cole was not an idol in my life; he was a model for my life."

He was not an idol in my life; he was a model for my life. Like **Hebrews 13:7** says, **"Remember your leaders, who spoke the word of God to you. Consider the outcome of their way of life and imitate their faith" (NIV).**

As men, we were never intended to be an island of independence. God wants us to link arms with other men to build a spiritual bridge that unites one generation to the next and one culture to another.

Dr. Cole taught that what *we resist grows weaker while what we submit to grows stronger.* If we want to strengthen our relationships with our pastor and mentor, we must lay aside all false pride and submit to them. After all, **Proverbs 18:12** tells us, **"Before his downfall a man is proud, but humility comes before honor."**

Like the cloud by day and fire by night, God will always be the One ultimately guiding and directing our life. However, when we find a "Moses" to lead the way, we should honor that man's life and leadership and cherish the time we have to learn from him.

The day will inevitably come when God says, **"Moses my servant is dead. Now then, you and all these people get ready to cross the Jordan" (Joshua 1:2).** Let's recognize and respect what we have before it's too late. Once he is gone, we must forge out our path without him.

God, I miss Dr. Ed Cole!

6

JUST DO IT!

**"You don't practice what you preach; you preach
what you practice."**

D r. Cole's daughter, Joann Cole Webster, wrote this
chapter. Dads, get ready to take notes!

Millions of people had the opportunity to see Ed Cole
in the pulpit. Three of us had the privilege of watching him
grow into it. Paul, Lois, and I lived for many summers in
a station wagon with the California license plate number
MJK054. As we played in the back, we didn't realize God
had given us a bird's eye view **of the making of a man**.
We watched and learned as our dad grew in spirit, drew an
appetite for the things of God, grew in hunger to see men
know Jesus, and grew into a great, gracious and Godly man.
Because of that, dad became more than just a natural father
to me. He became a spiritual father also, as I grew to understand the office God had given him to occupy in the Body
of Christ.

My earliest memories are of my mom and dad, brother
and sister, and in the little houses, station wagons, and

cramped motel rooms where we stayed while dad ministered. He was forever planning or talking about ministry. Nothing was more important to him than the Lord. Each Saturday night that he wasn't ministering somewhere else, dad will lay out all the families dress shoes on newspapers in the living room, and shine each pair. This was not just so his children would look good, but to teach by example how to value the Lord's assembly. One Sunday morning when he was home from evangelizing, he called to us from his bed and told us he was sick. He said this would be the first Sunday he had missed church since his salvation. It was a really, really big deal to him, and so it made a huge impression on us.

Besides the Lord, Dad loved our mom, and later would become well known for how he cherished his beloved Nancy. Next to his love for her, he loved us, and he showed it. I remember for my fourth birthday, he surprised me by creating a balloon dart throw in the garage. He loves sports, and we watched and rooted with him. He took us to miniature golf when he could afford it. He bought nuts in the shell that we would crack and eat together on winter holidays. He read to us from Scripture every night at "Family Altar". Because he made very little money ministering, he and mom were creative in entertaining and teaching us about values. Once Dad typed out the Ten Commandments on a white piece of paper, cut it in a circle, taped it to a piece of construction paper, and then taped it to the wall above my bed. It was a treasure, something he made just for me, and I read it every night.

Nothing seemed unusual to me about growing up with him. It was perfectly normal to trip over a cushion left in front of the chair, or a pillow left next to his bed – the vestiges remaining from his prayer life. His prayer times went like this – a pillow or cushion from the bed, chair, or couch went on the floor, under his knees. Another pillow went on the couch or chair back to press his head into. A blanket, bedspread or jacket went across his shoulders. The blanket was because he liked to stay warm while he prayed – perhaps a hold over from his early days. In his first years of pastoring in Sonora, California, he said he was too scared to preach, so he'd take my brother – a baby at the time – to the church altar with him and drape Paul over his shoulders while he prayed all Saturday night.

Once dad was in position, he would pray. Dad's prayer is usually started with a full voice. During my college years when I lived at home, he had regular prayer twice a day. First in the morning at the jetty in Newport Beach, California, then in the afternoon, sprawled facedown across boxes in the garage that were piled next to the garage door. I often came home in the afternoon and could hear his voice before I got out of my car. I would wonder what the mail carrier thought when he slipped the mail through the slot in Dad's garage door in the afternoons.

Dad's prayers were not confined to mornings or afternoons, to the beach or to the boxes, Dad prayed fervently and often, as the Spirit moved on him – breaking into prayer in the car, at the dinner table, or while playing with his grandchildren. We grew up listening to Mom and Dad's favorite albums, one of which was Mahalia Jackson who sang, "every time I feel the Spirit moving in my heart, I will pray." Dad lived that lyric. Throughout the day and night, at any time he felt moved, Dad would cry out where he was, or move into position, clutched the corners of a blanket to his chest and start out, "God my Father…." Almost always, the presence of God would immediately fill the place. The depth of dad's prayers and the overwhelming presence of the Lord God were amazing to me. I could've prayed for hours alongside him, and often did.

The strewn cushions and blanket were a mere physical evidence of Dad's prayers, but as the years passed, we began to see a greater evidence of those prayers in the depth and breadth of his ministry. It occurred almost without us noticing, while we kept growing up and just living our lives. Dad always said he preached for results, not reactions. On February 1-2, 1980, Paul was entrenched in his career in Christian television, Lois was in law school, and I was pursuing my undergrad degree, when Dad went to a men's retreat in the mountains of Oregon and preached a message that would go around the world, become his hallmark, and the basis for the book, *"Maximized Manhood."*

Ed Cole was slowly becoming something more than just "Dad." Men were drawn to him and to his message. He taught, *"You believe in the message because you believe in the man."* More than a million – perhaps multiple millions – of men came from all backgrounds and ethnicities to believe in Dad. People marveled at how he could attract such diversity, and leaders would often ask how he did it. But Dad didn't do it. He lived it. Dad never taught a lesson he had not lived. He said, *"Preach what you practice, don't just practice what you preach."*

At the memorial service held after Dad's burial, many people remarked to me about one small story I told in my eulogy. It was a vivid memory of traveling through the South and being hungry. There were no interstate freeways, no fast food, and Dad passed one highway restaurant after another looking for a place for the family to eat. Every place had a sign in the window prohibiting people of color. I couldn't read, so I just looked for the white square paper in the restaurant window. Each time I saw one I would beg Dad, just this once, to stop. *"I'm hungry, Daddy. Please stop."*

We finally found a restaurant and walked up the steps, only to see the sign yet again. Dad turned around and said we couldn't go in and explained why. A man and woman walked up the steps and saw us standing there – three skinny hungry kids, a worn out Mom, and a young balding Dad. When they heard Dad, they turned and got back in their car and left. Those people were some of the first to respond to the enormous wealth that sprang from the wells of wisdom Dad dug through study and prayer.

"You don't practice what you preach; you preach what you practice." And Dad did. So many examples – his prayer life, the way he treated my mother, the fact that he was still memorizing new passages of Scripture until two weeks before he left us to see the Lord, the way he pursued the mission God gave him, and the courage with which he and my Mom started over in ministry **in their fifties** with little more than a dream and determination. I was living with them when they started over, and served as their first employee, which meant I did everything.

At my house, I have a copy of the first job I ever did for my Dad. It was much earlier when I was five or six years old, and he let me stack up the copies of his first manuscript called, "The Mountains of Moses." I walked around a make-shift table in our four-room house, stacking papers, and Lois got to staple them. Twenty years later, I not only got to staple, but I got to write with my Dad. That job was my favorite. At first, we used two typewriters, then two computers, and finally two laptops.

Dad and I would write and rewrite, exchanging chapters or files or stacks of raw material, and our silence would drive my mother crazy. She would make us coffee, read her news-paper, and live her life in the next room. And at least one time during each week that we wrote, she would walk in, exasperated, and say, *"How can you two write a book together if you never talk?"* We'd look up from our computers, smile and wave, then stick our heads back down to work.

Usually, I'd type rough drafts to get Dad kick-started, he would rewrite it completely, I'd edit, and we'd go back and forth. But the final time through was always Dad's. When he would say, *"Don't touch it!"* I knew it was over, and as much as I wanted to fix a transition or clean something up, it was too late, that chapter was done.

This was when I began to realize who my Dad really was. More than just a guy, a minister, or an author, he was called of God to occupy a specific position during a specific time in history, and the office to which he was called was that of a prophet.

A prophet is known as much for his boldness in speaking unwelcome words as for his wisdom. Ed Cole was well known for both. With his prophetic edge, Dad could be a severe **critic**. When we worked and wrote together, he'd remark, *"Too wordy, Joann." "You can't say it that way Joann." "Jesus takes us from victory, Joann, not just to victory."*

From those carefully chosen words, truths sprang from God's own heart that embedded in the hearts of men worldwide. Men who lived out the principles Dad taught, taught him how to build a relationship. He "adopted" as sons those men in whom he saw the same spirit, which moved and motivated him. Many stayed with him to his end, but some did not.

Not everyone was enamored of being "cut," as G.F. Watkins calls it. Dad remained true to the call of God on his life, even as he was challenged, criticized, and occasionally censored. Such responses remind me of the passage from Luke about the rich young ruler who asked Jesus about eternal life. Jesus reminded him of the commandments. The young man said, **"All these have I kept from my youth up." Then Jesus said, "Yet lackest thou one thing; sell all that thou hast and distribute unto the poor, and thou shalt have treasure in heaven; and come, follow me." (Luke 18:21-22)**. The rich young ruler walked away sad. The young man thought he was doing everything right, by doing what he'd learned as a kid. But when he tried to convince Jesus, Jesus spoke a prophetic word to him.

Dad was many things to many men – **their mentor, father, grandfather, teacher, friend, and even commander. But**

to almost all, he was also a personal prophet, who would speak a word to us just when we thought we were doing something great, and he'd challenge us to rise to the next level. Then we had a decision to make. Get mad at him, get over it, or answer the challenge and get on with it.

It seems like in his absence, men still have a decision to make. They can be mad at the unpopular things he said. I know of no other author whose books have been thrown more often on the floor, against a cell wall, and across a room. Or they can walk away from his teachings sad like the rich young ruler, trying to get over it and forget the words spoken. Or, they can get on with it, and resolve to meet Dad's challenge.

Dad taught, "Fame can come in a moment, but greatness only comes with longevity." And he taught that Saul should have been proud of his servant David. Dad took what Saul had complained about in David and prophesied it over his spiritual "sons" and "daughters." He said where he got his thousands, we'll get our ten thousands.

Today, hunching over the couch and praying like my Dad is a joy to me. Not to please him, nor to gain his acceptance or love, because that season is over. Dad loved and accepted his kids, even if all we did was burp. The real reason I love to pray like my Dad is because I aspire to be like him, to answer the challenge to live the Christ-life.

Dad to me was my natural father, spiritual father, mentor, prophet and much more. Dad was my dictionary. Dad was my concordance. My pulpit commentary, encyclopedia of systematic theology, my Bible dictionary and my personal Bible answer-man. I aspire to be like him, because with Dad gone, I am aware more than ever of his uniqueness in the Body of Christ. Few have had a larger spirit than his. He remained larger than life to the end. In spite of Dad's human frailties and personal flaws, which we all have, God chose him to serve in the office of a prophet – a position within the Body of Christ that is worthy of deference, devotion and duty.

Of the millions who are still partaking of Dad's ministry, anyone can follow the same path and grow in spirit, in appetite for the things of God, in hunger to see men know Jesus, and into a great, gracious and Godly person. The world is dimmer in the absence of his passionate and generous spirit. It is up to us to fill the world once more with the light he was given.

The message Dad preached about Christlikeness is the message he lived. It was an honor to hear him preach, an honor to watch him pray, an honor to serve at his side, and an honor to support the ministry the Lord accomplished through his life. It would have been an honor just to have shaken his hand.

"You don't practice what you preach; you preach what you practice."

7

INCREASE

**"God cannot make an able man faithful, but
He can make a faithful man able."**

I recently watched a television program about "eight minute dating"- the latest social trend. I had never heard of it before, but I was intrigued with what I saw. Single men and women arrive at a designated meeting place with a list of two or three questions they want to ask members of the opposite sex. Each man is seated at a table with a woman and the interview begins. Questions are asked, answers are exchanged, and impressions quickly written down before the eight-minute timer indicates that it's time to change stations. Each man then meets a different woman, and they invest eight minutes into each other before writing "yea" or "nay" on their comment card. At the end of the night, after multiple "eight-minute dates," cards are collected and compared. If a match can be made, there is a chance for a second date.

In a time-conscience society, we hate to invest time into anything, even people, unless we can be sure we'll get something out if it. Most Americans will admit it is a daily battle to find balance, and the things we profess as priorities often take a backseat to the routine demands of everyday life. If we're not careful, quality time with our family is reduced to a goodnight kiss and our prayer time becomes a few words of thanks as our head hits the pillow. Unfortunately, the things that matter most often get the least amount of time and attention. Furthermore, if we wait until we have time to reprioritize our life, we never will.

Dr. Cole taught me a simple way to quickly identify a man's priorities. A person's day-timer and checkbook tell us all we need to know about their main concerns in life. No matter what we say we value most, what we spend the majority of our time and money on is what really matters to us.

Based on this test, do a quick self-evaluation, and determine what in life is most important to you.

DR. COLE'S EXAMPLE

While there are numerous fathering models out there and many men who refer to themselves as spiritual fathers, Dr. Cole exemplified an essential ingredient that cannot be left out of genuine fatherhood. Dr. Cole made himself available to me. He was willing to invest time in me. He not only welcomed me to contact him anytime for anything, he kept in touch with me as well. He actually called me quite frequently despite his hectic ministry schedule. He did more than speak Biblical truths to me; he extended a caring hand, and took sincere interest in my life.

> *No matter what we say we value most, what we spend the majority of our time and money on is what really matters to us.*

Have you ever noticed male conversations almost always start and end with occupational details? Even pastors tend to discuss the well being of the ministry, church attendance, secured speaking engagements, and all the other pastoral achievements worth mentioning. It's not a bad trait in men. God made us laborers and providers, and we take pride in that. It's just that this usual trend made my conversations with Dr. Cole all the more rare and unique. While he did express an interest in my ministry, he was always much more concerned with my marriage and family to make sure I was balanced. He preferred to ask about my children and spend time discussing the more personal issues in my life, rather then ministerial affairs. He honestly cared about the quality of

A father is truly concerned with the fulfillment of his children and the deeper issues in their life.

my life as much as the accomplishments of my occupation. That was invaluable to me, because that is the heart of a father. This was a pivotal point in my decision to claim him as my spiritual father.

A *master* **only desires production from his servants, and a** *teacher* **is satisfied when his student passes the test; however, a** *father* **is truly concerned with the** *fulfillment* **of his children and the deeper issues in their life**. While a father applauds his son's academic and occupational successes, he finds the greatest joy sharing his personal victories. That is how Dr. Cole cared for me, and this method of fatherhood is what I now seek to emulate for the men in my church. I pray that every leader who reads this book will do the same.

The following is a letter Dr. Cole personally wrote to me after I ministered for him at the Heart of the Lion Conference in May of 2002. I believe it captures the heart of the father and illustrates the benefits of becoming a son:

Dear G.F.,

> *Well, what can I say except that your message was absolutely exceptional! It's regrettable*

that you did not have two hours to minister it in, but on the other hand, it was good that you stopped when you did, because it had the people leave wanting more. And that's always a good thing to do.

Your demonstration of Jesus being raised by Joseph brought home an earthly living and lifestyle that Jesus must have been raised in. It conveyed to all of us the importance of the Son- even Jesus- being raised by a father. You capped off "Build Men and Raise Sons" better than anything I could have imagined.

Thank you for your exceptional ministry. Everyone at Heart of the Lion was blessed beyond measure from it.

You continue to grow in faith and in stature with God and man, and it's amazing to see it. Surely any apostolic signs of ministry are becoming evident in you. As you continue to humble yourself and let the Holy Ghost work in you, it will show itself more and more as it begins to touch more and more nations.

You and Rose make a great team. And you're right to complement her and promote her as you do because she's growing at pace with you. Her ministry was a blessed one at Heart of the Lion.

G.F., I love you. I enjoy being around you, having fellowship with you, listening to you, and just imbibing your infectious, enthusiastic, anointed lifestyle. May you ever continue to grow in stature and in favor with God and man as you grow in Christ. You're wonderful to watch, and I praise God for you.

Thank you for your friendship. It's a gift of God, and I treasure and esteem it with the highest of value.

Keep in touch, because I want to be.

Your in Christ for Christ
Edwin Louis Cole

Dr. Ed Cole believed in me. He affirmed my calling like no other man. It was not until Jesus, our great example, was thirty years old that his father affirmed him in front of witnesses at the Jordan River. After the heaven opened and God's voice was heard "This is my son in whom I am well pleased," the miracles in Jesus' life began. Likewise, when your spiritual father affirms you, your calling and miracles will manifest.

A FORMULA FOR VICTORY

There is a certain pattern I see repeatedly in the Bible and have also experienced in my own life. **Relationship brings revelation, revelation brings faith, and faith brings victory!**

Relationship brings revelation, revelation brings faith, and faith brings victory!

When we say we know someone, we aren't saying much. Most Americans know who Jesus is, but they do not know Him personally. Consequently, they know He came to the Earth, but they don't know why He came.

79

They've heard history's account of His compassion for humanity, but they don't know how He feels about them as an individual. They can conclude that He died on a cross, but they don't know what motivated Him to do it. They do not have *revelation* about Jesus because they have never entered into *relationship* with Him.

Relationship brings revelation. When I have revelation, I know more than when and what; I also know why and how. If we are ever going to **do the works that Jesus did and even greater (John 14:12),** we have to go beyond when and what He did and know why and how He did it. We have to progress from logos to rhema, from head knowledge to heart knowledge, and from religion to relationship.

I knew who Dr. Cole was through books and tapes before I knew him personally; however, it was only when we had relationship that I realized why and how he did what he did, which revolutionized my life. Dr. Cole's willingness to avail himself to me allowed us to develop a relationship, which leads to revelation, which brought faith, and faith made victory possible!

FAITHFULNESS

I remember walking into Dr. Cole's hotel room in Longview, Texas. I had no idea at the time that this was one of the last ministry engagements I would spend with him. He laid down on the bed to rest his back and motioned for me to sit down bedside him. He talked about several things, and as always, his words meant a great deal to me. I cherished the moments I had his undivided attention, as every natural and spiritual son does. As our conversation progressed, Dr. Cole told me of his plans to minister in Singapore. He seemed very passionate about making the trip, and it was obviously extremely very important to him. He went on to say that he wanted me to go with him, an invitation I was honored to receive. There was just one problem. The date of the trip conflicted with an oversees ministry engagement of my own. We had already purchased the plane tickets and plans were already underway for a big men's event we were spearheading in South Africa and Scotland. Pastors and men were expecting us, and thousands of dollars had already been spent.

My heart felt heavy as I told Dr. Cole of my conflict, but I will never forget his response to my dilemma. He pointed at me with that famous bent finger and said, "G.F. you'll go to Africa again, but this is my last trip to Singapore." It was at that moment that I fully realized what it meant to be a son. How could I call myself a real son and not fulfill my father's desires when it was in my power to do so? It's easy to call ourselves sons when we are receiving all the benefits of our father's advice and love; however, it's another thing to remain a son when it requires sacrifice on our part.

I came home and prepared my secretary and staff for a change of plans. We made arrangements for two of my mentored men to fly to South Africa and conduct the meetings so that I could go to Singapore. It just so happened that health complications required Dr. Cole to cancel his trip, but my conscience was clear. I felt good that I would have been there if he had gone.

Proverbs 20:6 tells us many will say that they are loyal friends, but who can find one who is really **faithful**?" Dr. Cole availed himself to me, and in return, I made a decision to be faithful to him. I was committed to honor him as a father and esteem him above myself, and I believe Dr. Cole was blessed by that, and I know I certainly was!

JOSEPH'S EXAMPLE

It's amazing to think how much society has changed since Jesus walked the earth. Jesus never used a cell phone, sent a fax, or placed an online order. There was no website advertising His next ministry engagement, no microphones for His sermon on the Mount, and no subway to take Him from Nazareth to Galilee. Jesus did not have the convenience of modern technology, but He went to work with something far greater than a laptop. He went to work with Joseph, His father.

Day after day, year after year, Jesus spent time in the carpenter's shop with Joseph. Where do you think Jesus came up with His parables about tress, lamps, oxen, yokes, and seeds? His stepfather, Joseph, trained his son by using the natural elements he could see, to teach him spiritual truths that could not be seen. As we come to understand natural laws, it becomes easier to understand spiritual laws. Like **1 Corinthians 15:46** says, **"First the natural and then the spiritual."**

Joseph was building far more than cabinets in that carpenter's shop; he was reinforcing character, trustworthiness, integrity, and holiness in Jesus. Just like God handpicked Mary to be Jesus's mother, He carefully chose Joseph to be Jesus' earthly father. Can you imagine being the man responsible to set the example of manhood for Jesus Christ? Even though we don't hear much about Joseph after the second chapter of Luke, we know what kind of parent he was as we watch the life of Jesus.

Proverbs 22:6 says, **"Train up a child in the way he should go and when he is old he will not depart from it."** I believe Jesus learned obedience and sacrifice from Joseph. He could have put Mary away when he discovered she was pregnant; however, he chose to obey God, marry her, and take responsibility for a child that was not his own. He chose God's will over his own.

The same obedience and sacrifice we see in Joseph, we also see in Jesus in the Garden of Gethsemane when He prayed, **"Not my will, but thine be done"** **(Luke 22:42).** He kept His commitment to God and took responsibility for sins that were not His own.

Jesus was not Joseph's biological son, but that did not keep Joseph from loving Him with heart of a father. Likewise, we can become spiritual fathers in the faith as soon as we get past the mindset, *"he's not my son; he's not my responsibility."* It's not about relatives; it's about relationship. Like **1 Corinthians 4:15** says, **"We have plenty of instructors; it's fathers that are hard to come by."** Consider the following testimony by Jack King, Associate Minister with Dr. Cole for over 15 years, as well as the Founder and President of Faithful Men's Ministries:

Jesus was not Joseph's biological son, but that did not keep joseph from loving Him with the heart of a father.

Dr. Cole saved my life. The first time I heard Dr. Cole, he was teaching on the principle of release and forgiveness from John 20:22, 23. I had accepted Christ just a short time before this meeting.

Just a few years prior to this, my father had been murdered, "Execution Style," the headlines screamed. That night, as I held his lifeless body in my arms, I made a vow to him that I would avenge his death and bring his murderer to justice. The murder investigation lasted almost 2 years, and we successfully identified the man who plotted and arranged my father's death. Unfortunately, damaged evidence prevented legal sentencing, and despite the testimony of several witnesses, the man was never charged. I began pursuing a grand jury petition to get his case reinstated. It was going to be my last legal effect before I was going to take matters into my own hands and fulfill the vow I made to my dad. Somehow, someway, the man that had him murdered him was going to have to pay for it.

But God had other plans for my life. Through a friend of mine, I came to accept Christ as my Lord and Savior. At that moment of complete transformation of my heart and life, God took every bit of hate, anger, and vengeance out of my heart. I couldn't believe that I had no more desire to pursue my father's case. I knew God had changed my life. Then that same friend invited me to a meeting where Ed Cole was preaching.

Dr. Cole was teaching about how Jesus was telling the disciples about releasing other's sins out of your life and the consequences when you don't. He quoted Jesus saying, **"If you don't forgive those who sin against you, you will retain their sin in your life" (John 20:23).** Dr. Cole stopped and looked at the audience and said, *"If there's someone in your life that you have not been able to forgive, then get out of your seat and get down to the altar."* Dr. Cole wanted to pray God's Words that says He will cleanse us from those unrighteous things that have been done to us **(1 John 1:9).**

Dr. Cole continued to speak as men came forward. I remember him saying, *"If you walk in unforgiveness, you make yourself greater than God because He has never walked in unforgiveness."*

That statement broke my heart when I realized God might think that I thought I was greater than Him because I had not forgiven the man that had my dad murdered. I couldn't get out of my seat and down the steps to the altar quick enough!

Dr. Cole began praying for the men. When he came to me and prayed, I released the sin of murder and released that man's sin out of my life. What a release and freedom I experienced. **"Whom the Son set free is free indeed" (John 8:36).**

When I tuned to go back to my seat, the Lord spoke something to me that was the beginning of my real Christian walk as a man of God. I heard the Lord say, *"Now go to the man that you have hunted, and ask him to forgive you."* I thought God had it backwards! I thought He meant I should go to the man and tell him I forgive him. The Lord just repeated it to me again, *"Go to that man and ask him to forgive you."* I realized if this were to happen in my life, it would have to be God! I sat in my seat and told God there is no way I could do what He was asking me to do. Basically I told God, I can't! He then told me His grace would be sufficient- and it was.

God brought this man across my path and not only was I able, by God's grace, to ask him to forgive me, but God allowed me to lead this man to the Lord. What jubilation in my heart when he accepted Christ. That night was when God spoke to me again and said He could now launch me in the direction he had created me to go.

A short time later, Dr. Cole called me and asked me to come work for his ministry. That was a little over 25 years ago. It was wonderful to serve him, pray with him, and be mentored by him. He was an incredible man to work for, but he was more than a boss. He treated me like a son. He became the father I lost.

A few months before Dr. Cole went home to be with the Lord, he called me to his home and gave me his notes from the meeting he taught on the principle of release- forgiveness. As I wrapped my arms around him to hug him, I realized God had avenged my father's death. He gave me Ed Cole to be my spiritual father.

That night, many years ago at Ed Cole's meeting, is when my life in Christ really began. It was the night Ed Cole saved my life!

SURROGATE SPIRITUAL FATHERS

Society has drastically changed over the centuries, but the human heart has remained the same. We still need the security and identity we gain from spending quality time with our father. Unfortunately, research has shown that in the homes that do have fathers, the average American man gives just 35 seconds of undivided attention to his children a day! As a result, most of us do not receive adequate spiritual guidance and instruction from our biological fathers. That is why there is such a need in the Body of Christ for "surrogate" fathers in the faith.

Discipleship relationships require that we give of our time. It's our job to search our own heart and take an internal inventory. Are we investing time in people? Are we available to others? Are we faithful to those who invest in us? Talent and gifts are not a sign of spiritual maturity; faithfulness is. God can make a faithful man able, but he cannot make an able man faithful.

Talent and gifts are not a sign of spiritual maturity; faithfulness is.

Faithfulness is the foundation strong relationships are built on and is one of the most meaningful gifts we can give our father. It's the kind of gift he won't necessarily ask for but would love to receive. We must purpose in our heart to give our fathers the gift of faithfulness and allow the process to bring us to new levels as a man, minister, husband, and spiritual father.

God, I miss that man.

8

BUILDING RELATIONSHIPS

~~~

"Gratitude confirms relationships."

This chapter was written by another one of Dr. Cole's sons of the faith, my good friend – Pastor Robert Barringer. He has spent the last 20 years as a missionary in Lima, Peru, where he has established two orphanages, two shelters for battered women, and a Bible seminary school. Robert and his wife Karyn also pastor a thriving 6,000-member church.

"Honor thy father and mother; [which is the first commandment with a promise] That it may be well with thee, and thou mayest live long on the earth" (Ephesians 6:2-3 KJV)

This one commandment comes with a promise: Honor your father and mother. The rewards are a good and long life. We can have a long life, but not necessarily a good life. Long life may not be desirable if it is a life that goes bad. God's promise is a long, good life. God has given us His principles and patterns by which to live and on which to build. If we live and build according to His pattern, His promise is that our life and our ministry life will be good and long.

The word "honor" literally translates in Hebrew as "heavy" (Kabed, 'kaw-bade'; a primitive root; to be heavy).

The best way to explain what "heavy" means within the word honor is to look at the opposite, which is "light." To take something lightly can be a form of dishonor. We dishonor our parents by taking our God ordained relationship with them lightly.

"For though ye have ten thousand instructors in Christ yet have ye not many fathers" (1 Corinthians 4:15 KJV). The problem in today's world is that we do not have a good idea of the role of a father because there is a lack of fathers – physically in the home and spiritually in the church.

I never knew my natural father throughout my childhood. He left my life when I was six months old, yet the Bible does not say to honor only good fathers. The promise is that if we honor our father, we will have a long, good life.

We dishonor our parents by taking our God-ordained relationship with them lightly.

Not having had a natural father as a role model, the Lord has blessed my life with spiritual fathers, for which I am thankful. We are to honor that spiritual fathering relationship as well. To take lightly your relationship with your spiritual father is, in a sense, dishonor. By putting the proper weight to honoring our pastors and our spiritual fathers, the same promise holds true – that we will have a long life, or a long-lived ministry life that goes well.

Scripture states that wisdom builds a house. Scripture also states that we need wise counsel. So, to gain the wisdom we need to build our houses, we need wise, fatherly counselors. One of the spiritual fathers in my life was Edwin Louis Cole. I read his books and showed his teachings on a television station in Lima, Peru. Though I did not know him personally, his ministry blessed my family and our church. So I sought after his teaching, and the possibility of a visit to our country. Through circumstances that only the Lord can ordain, a "chance" meeting came with

Roger Leyton, whose ministry worked with Dr. Cole in Central America, and another "chance" meeting occurred with Dr. Cole's son Paul in a conference in Los Angeles.

Dr. Cole was soon on his way to minister in Peru. When Dr. Cole came to minister at our church, we didn't take it lightly. We showed appreciation and readily received his message. And as a result Dr. Cole poured more into us. Our honor toward Dr.

We learned to show honor by being thankful.

Cole during that visit developed into a fathering relationship. **Every minister enjoys ministering to people who are appreciative and show gratitude.** A mentoring relationship developed, and new life was added to our ministry – good life.

Today, the leadership team often regards our church as "before Cole" and "after Cole" because we were fathered by Dr. Cole and applied the principles that he taught us. Dr. Cole had an amazing ability to expand a person's way of thinking. He made every "son" in the faith feel special. For example, Dr. Cole often told me, "Don't limit God." Circumstances had run our ministry for too long. But Dr. Cole had a way of increasing the man, to make us think bigger and believe for more. We started using the curriculum he wrote for the *Maximized Manhood* book and our church grew from 500 to 5,000 in 5 years. We attribute much of this growth to Dr. Cole's ministry.

Gratitude is a sign of relationship. Dr. Cole taught us, *"Gratitude confirms relationships."* We learned to show honor by being thankful. After Jesus healed them, nine lepers were healed and walked away. They showed no desire for a further relationship with Jesus. One came back and showed gratitude for his healing. Gratitude shows appreciation and value, so our expression of thankfulness to Dr. Cole honored him. By honoring him, it increased our lives and ministry.

It's a valuable lesson – thankfulness and gratitude show honor, by gratitude a relationship is developed, and life is added to that relationship.

On the other hand, taking lightly the things we receive from a ministry shows dishonor. Life will be taken away from the blessing we could have received. If we seek after men of wisdom, those with a father's heart, and receive their teachings, we must also show them honor by being thankful as they help to build our lives. I noticed during Dr. Cole's lifetime that many who were close to him took lightly that relationship. They loved him and said they honored him, but they did not give the relationship the proper weight.

Once I asked Dr. Cole about a minister that had been close to him. I was humbled by all of the attention Dr. Cole poured into my family and our church in the latter years of his life. When I asked Dr. Cole why he poured so much into us, and seemed cool toward the other ministry, his response was, *"When I go there, I feel as though I represent him."* In other words, he was being used as a "name," but there was no lasting relationship and ministry going on. That ministry took lightly Dr. Cole's gift, and because of that they never gained the full benefit of that relationship.

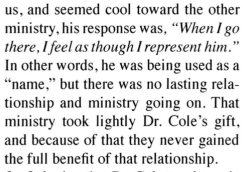

Every father provides three things for his children- security, identity, and provision.

Part of the pattern for fathering that Dr. Cole taught us, is that every father provides three things for his children – **security, identity, and provision**. Children who grow up without a good father in the home can grow up insecure. Fathers bring security to a family. The same principle works on a spiritual level. I know of many pastors who have never had a spiritual father, or a mentor, and as a result they are insecure in their ministry.

Children that grow up without a father in the home lack identity. We were taught that street gangs and men's social clubs are just substitute families. To some men, their identity is in a sports club, baseball team, or football game. When children do not find their identity in the home, they look for identity some place else. If they don't find their identity in the structure of the home, they will look toward the gangs or the subcultures of rock music, drugs, or sports. The father can bring identity to the home.

When kids do not find identity in the home, they look for identity some place else.

The same way that the father brings identity to the natural home, spiritual fathers bring identity to their spiritual sons. I can proudly say that I was one of the spiritual sons of Dr. Edwin Louis Cole. By identifying with a spiritual father, this brought identity to our church family. The church family felt secure in this identity, knowing that there was a spiritual father speaking into their pastor.

Fathers also provide provision, in particular when, through them, the curse is lifted from the earth. **"And he shall turn the heart of the fathers to the children, and the heart of the children to their fathers, lest I come and smite the earth with a curse" (Malachi 4:6 KJV).** Why does it not say that he will return the hearts to the mothers? Pastor Lafayette Scales has said in ministry that the hearts of the mothers are naturally turned to the children. It is the father's hearts that have drifted away from the children.

Malachi added, **"Lest I come and smite the earth with a curse."** According to this passage, the healing for the curse on the nations today is fathers who take the place that the Lord ordained for them and sons who honor them. Then there is healing in the land.

One reason the Church is unhealthy is because the hearts of the spiritual sons have been distant from their spiritual fathers. There are times when one will look at their pastor or leaders in ministry and not see past their human (flesh) side.

The sin of familiarity sets in. Seeing the human side of a man's ministry can cause us to take his ministry lightly. This is dishonor, and it hinders us from fathering relationships.

Another way a father provides is by making room for their sons. There is always room at our father's house. "There is plenty of room for you in my Father's home. If that weren't so, would I have told you that I'm on my way to get a room ready for you?" (John 14:2). The family of God is amazing in that there is room for everyone: room to grow, room to minister, and a place where sons can fulfill their destiny.

Dr. Cole had the ability to make every son feel special. There was a place for everyone. My son, Taylor, had to do a summer internship for his college degree so he chose to work for Dr. Cole in his ministry in Dallas. Taylor decided to extend his stay and miss an entire semester in college, because Dr. Cole's health had declined. Taylor wanted to stay with him, "until the chariot took him home." Dr. Cole had not only become a father to me, but he had become a grandfather to my two children.

On Monday, August 26, 2002, Taylor called me at our home in Lima to say they had taken Dr. Cole to the hospital. I caught the first flight to Dallas, arrived Tuesday morning, and went straight to the hospital where Dr. Cole rested in the intensive care unit. There I realized something. Not only did Dr. Cole have a huge heart, but he had taught his three children to have big hearts as well. His daughter Joann insisted that Taylor and I spend time alone with Dr. Cole, just as each of Dr. Cole's children did with their families while he was holding on to his last minutes of life. We did. We cried. We prayed together.

At 3:15pm, his son Paul came out of the intensive care room with the family gathered around and announced that Dr. Cole went home. Taylor and I stayed together and prayed trying to give the family space, but the family would have none of it. Paul, Lois, and Joann – the three natural children – made us all feel like we were part of their family. I was there to honor my spiritual father and be with my son. This honor built a place for me with the family.

When the memorial service was held later in Dallas, many people testified of what the Lord had done through Dr. Cole's ministry. It was a time of rejoicing. But when the family stood up toward the end of the service, they called Taylor to stand with them. They said Dr. Cole had nine grandchildren, and then presented my son with one of Dr. Cole's favorite jackets. They had embroidered a number "10" on it, and declared that Taylor was "Grandchild Number Ten." He was adopted into the family. Once again I was amazed at the bigness of their house.

In a true father's house, there is provision, and there is room: room to grow, to be a part, and to fulfill one's destiny. Only after Dr. Cole's departure from this earth did I realize that with him it was simple – if we drew close to him, there was room for us. This is a huge example for me because now I am a spiritual father. I have over 100-orphaned children and hundreds of young pastors I take care of, and I know it is possible for me to make room for them, each one.

As men look ahead to the future without this great leader of men, Ed Cole, let us not remove the foundations that our fathers have laid before us. We must take those foundations and move on, that it may go well with us and that there may be health in the land.

9

THE ART OF COMMUNICATION

"The art of communication is based on listening."

At just three years of age, J.F.K. Jr. watched from the curb as his father's funeral procession went by. He was most likely too young to comprehend that President Kennedy's casket, containing the lifeless body of his father, was just a few feet away. What he did recognize, however, was the red, white, and blue symbol draped over the casket. Without hesitation, he raised his hand to salute our nation's flag. The image of the small boy honoring his father's legacy remains one of the most famous pictures ever taken of J.F.K. Jr.

Patriotism is not *taught*; it's *caught*. J.F.K. Jr. *caught* his father's spirit. The respect he had for the American flag was birthed out of his father's love for the American people. When President Kennedy no longer stood, what he stood for was well alive in the heart of his son.

History continually provides us with examples of fathers who dramatically influenced and impacted their sons. Where would President George W. Bush Jr. be without his father's mentorship? He obviously caught his father's spirit and it took him all the way to the White House. Likewise, John Quincy Adams instilled a political passion in his son and they too served separate terms as President of the United States.

What about sports legends like the infamous speed racer, Mario Andretti? His sons now blaze down the track and are winning trophies of their own. His grandson, Marco, is also excelling in the sport. Mario Andretti not only taught his sons how to drive, he impressed in them a passion to win!

CATCHING MY FATHER'S SPIRIT

More is caught than taught.

Have you ever noticed we often learn how to do something correctly only after we've experienced doing it the wrong way? I was right in the middle of doing things the wrong way when God intervened and showed me the proper means to honor and relate to Dr. Cole.

I realized that during my many early conversations with Dr. Cole, I continually spoke about a certain topic – *me*! I found myself going on and on about *my* challenges, *my* church, *my* concerns and *my* victories. What perplexed me was when I would get about halfway through my monologue, Dr. Cole would interject a few points and then change the subject. I knew he cared about my life, but I also knew he was a focused man.

What God instilled in me through this experience is that more is *caught* than *taught*. If I spent more time listening to what Dr. Cole had to say, versus focusing on what I thought he needed to hear about my circumstances, the majority of my questions would have been answered. It was at that point that I came to understand the power of impartation, something I am convinced many sons know very little about.

We must strive to catch our father's *spirit*, not just his *solutions*. When you catch his spirit, the solutions become evident. I had to grasp the patterns and principles Dr. Cole lived his life by and gain understanding as to why he did what he did. The only way to do that was to shut my mouth and allow him to impart his spiritual seed, his words, into my life. His words were derived out of years of experience and decades of prayer.

Dr. Cole's endorsements and involvement with our ministry was not the only driving force behind the ministerial success we've experienced at PowerHouse Church. It was when I applied his same patterns and princi-

> *We must strive to catch our father's spirit, not just his solutions.*

ples that we began to see increases and favor on our ministry.

THE TRIP I'LL NEVER FORGET

I still remember being elated that Dr. Cole would ask me to accompany him on a ministry trip. I had been to Promise Keepers events in the past, but never alongside one of the premier speakers! After checking into the hotel, I was privileged to meet Coach McCartney, the Founder of Promise Keepers. I was surprised to learn that he attributed his salvation experience and a great deal of his spiritual growth, to the influence of Dr. Cole, whom he referred to as his mentor. I met many pastors and men's ministry leaders that day, and felt honored to be there.

Dr. Cole and I sat in box seats at the New Jersey Continental Arena and listened to a great speaker deliver a powerful message before Dr. Cole asked me to get up and go away with him. It was just one hour before Dr. Cole was to take the stage so I escorted him outside. *"G.F., let's pray,"* he said, and that's exactly what we did for the next 40 or so minutes. He simply walked around praying in the Spirit as I walked behind him, praying what he prayed, and agreeing with what he said.

It just so happened that the entrance gate to the Convention Center was within an eye's view of where we were. Long lines of men with tickets in hand were amazed when they recognized Dr. Cole praying close by. While Dr. Cole always seemed oblivious to the popularity he managed to attract over the years, the men stared, pointed and admired their "hero" as they went by. They began quoting "Coleisms" and shouting, *"1,2,3, yes!"* Some men said things like, *"You've changed my life Dr. Cole,"* and *"Thank you Dr. Cole!"* They had read his books, attended his meetings, and gained a great respect for him. He represented what we all want to be, a maximized and Christ-like man, and they were obviously thrilled and awestruck to see him.

I'll say one thing about Dr. Cole – he sure knew how to pray! We had a powerful time of intercession outside that day. After he brought down Heaven and bound up hell, he grabbed my hands and we began praying in the Spirit together – really loud!

We entered the stadium and it was time for Dr. Cole to take the stage. He was the second speaker to appear before the 22,000 men that day. The man who spoke before him delivered a dynamic salvation message and some 5,000 men had just responded to an altar call to make Jesus their Lord and Savior!

In Dr. Cole's unusual straightforward fashion, he took the microphone commanding the men to repent of their sex sins. After a short message, he opened up the altars for every man struggling in the area of sexual purity to come forward. Some 7,000 men left the comfort of their seats, weeping and repenting to the Lord. It was a supernatural sight.

THE FLIGHT HOME

So there I was, sitting next to Dr. Cole, cherishing every minute of our flight home. I couldn't help but reflect on all the places he had been, the people he had know, the Generals he had touched, and the lives God had changed through him. He laid there peacefully, blowing air bubbles and dreaming.

He woke up periodically, said a word or two as I listened intently. People all over the world, myself included, had come to him with their life story and he patiently listened to their plea for advice. I had finally learned to just be quiet and listen, to get out of my world long enough to spend some time in his. He seemed to appreciate that.

I clearly remember one specific statement he made as he woke from his nap. He looked at me and said, *"G.F., do you know how to define the word nagging?"* I thought he was about to share a wealth of spiritual information and Scriptures so I took out my notepad and pen and said, *"No sir, I don't."* He said, *"The definition of nagging is being right at the wrong time."* His clever observation was followed by a hearty belly laugh and I realized he was actually telling a joke (though it was a truth I have since quoted on many occasions).

Sitting next to Dr. Cole on that plane was a defining moment for me. He was just being himself, telling a joke, laughing with a friend. I was truly privileged to be there. It was not only what he said that day that made an impression on me, but also his actions. Again, more is caught than taught. I remember how kind and caring he was to the stewardess that day. He took the time to say uplifting things to her and acknowledged her importance, all of which had an obvious encouraging effect on her. He was always so debonair and had such control over his vocabulary. I watched how he greeted people and brought a smile to their face. He had a genuine love and concern for the well being of others, loved ones and strangers alike.

My administrative assistant once commented that every time Dr. Cole called the office, she tried to connect him to me as quickly as possible out of respect for him and his time. However, he never let her transfer the call before he would comment, *"How are you doing today? How is your Family? I've enjoyed talking with you. Thanks for your assistance."*

I was also able to spend quality time with Dr. Cole traveling to and from New Jersey during that event and at our hotel. It meant a great deal to me to have access to his life those few hours. I learned a lot from watching and listening to Dr. Cole on that trip. It was supernatural for me.

FAMILIARITY BREEDS CONTEMPT

It was always a treat to be around Dr. Cole, to glean from him, and take advantage of every benefit of spiritual sonship. However, God taught me early on that *familiarity breeds contempt*. I purposed in my heart that I wanted Dr. Cole to be a spiritual father in my life: someone I could always receive from. I've learned through my years as a coach, principal, and now pastor, that there's a point, a line, that can be crossed where people no longer receive from us as an authority figure in their life. That's why Jesus said he could do no mighty works in His hometown (Matthew 15:38), because the people considered Him common and familiar. They knew Him after the flesh, but they did not recognize who He was in the Spirit. They failed to discern His purpose in their lives.

Since I identified Dr. Cole as a "pearl of great price," a gem to be valued and respected, I never pursued a "best friend" relationship with him. Maintaining an attitude of a spiritual son ensured there would be no room for offense when he spoke character-building truths into my life.

Spiritual fathers are not in our life to be our best friend.

It wasn't always easy to resist the urge to take our relationship to a more relaxed and friendly level. Even though Dr. Cole called me several times a month, there were seasons in my life when I wanted to call him every single day. As a matter of fact, what I really wanted to do was hop on a plane and show up at his doorstep! Would he have allowed me to call and visit so often? Of course he would have; that's the heart of a father. However, I stuck to the decision to guard that relationship and allow a certain amount of needed distance. It is the subordinate's job, the son's responsibility, to keep the relationship on a level of respect.

Spiritual fathers are not in our life to be our best friend. We should give fathers the liberty to "cut" us with life-sobering truths and speak the hard things so we can grow up. Spiritual fathers disciple; this involves discipline. Proverbs 13:24 tells us if we love our son, we have to discipline him. While fathers are a vital source of support, they also need the liberty to critique us when we're in need of direction and counsel.

A tree does not grow to its fullest unless it's pruned. Neither do we. While we never like for the coach to point out our mistakes, it's the only way we quit making them. Furthermore, when we make it to the end zone, we're suddenly grateful for his honest intervention.

In the world today, almost any fact or figure can be found at our fingertips. We can access millions of answers on the "information highway," the Internet, but that's not where we get answers to life's most important issues. We find character, maturity and spiritual fortitude during those significant moments spent with our father. When we spend hours, days and years submitted to their mentorship, the information hidden in their heart becomes an impartation into our life and the navigation for our future.

History proves that in times past it was the father's job to teach his sons a trade. From boyhood to manhood, sons worked side by side with their father, gleaning both natural and spiritual skill sets. Unfortunately, present day society is no longer structured that way. Public schools and universities compete for a father's time and attention. As valuable as an education is, we cannot allow it, or any other variable, to disconnect us from our children. They need to catch our spirit. They need to have a time of understanding or standing under.

One of the men I mentor submitted the following testimony about his father:

> My grandfather died when my father was just a little boy. Consequently, my father grew up without an example and model of true manhood. Although I know he loved my siblings and I very much, he was never able to express and communicate his approval and affection for us. We had a distant relationship with him since his primary focus was simply being the breadwinner.
>
> Through the mentoring process and Dr. Cole's curriculum, I have learned how to be a better father to my sons, a more attractive husband to my wife, and a significant source of care and direction for my friends in Christ. I now know what it takes to be a man of integrity, and I have purposed in my heart to teach others what my mentor has effectively taught me. His words have transformed my life and the effect of that will be seen throughout the generations to come.

James 1:19 tells us to be "quick to hear but slow to speak". When we're with those we love, we should spend less time talking and more time listening. The art of communication is based on listening.

When I learned to talk less and listen more to Dr. Cole, I tapped into the highest level of discipleship I had ever know. Think about it, God made you with two ears and one mouth. You think He was trying to make a point about listening twice as much as speaking?

God, I miss that man!

10

THE MENTORED MARRIAGE

"Your ministry is only as strong as your marriage."

I t never fails. Every time a couple enters a new level of leadership in our church, new challenges seem to flood their home. Like clockwork, spiritual *promotion* is followed by spiritual *commotion*. That's because the devil knows that when the pressures of life are applied, a marriage will often divide. **"A house divided will never stand" (Mark 3:25).** If he can divide a husband and wife ministry team, he can devour their ministry. He attacks our covenant relationships in an attempt to distract us from our calling. What an effective strategy the devil has developed.

How can we run with a vision when we're in division with our life partner? How can we expect diverse cultures, different races, and varying denominations to make peace with one another when we can't even get along with our spouse in our own home? Our covenant (first with God, then with our spouse) is the foundation: the concrete slab that all ministries are built on. When it cracks, the structure we have labored to build shifts and often collapses. In all actuality, our marriage is our primary ministry. I'll never forget when Dr. Cole asked my wife and I, "*If you really want to be out-standing pastors and raise up a successful ministry, do you know what one thing you must do?"* With our eyes focused and fixed on Dr. Cole while Rose and I both answered, *"No sir, what?"* He said, *" You must put your marriage first. Take out your day-timers and write down, in advance, what days you will set aside for dates and quality time together. Only after you have scheduled time together for each other should you go back and pencil in church functions. Protect the dates you've reserved for each other, because your ministry is only as strong as your marriage."*

That simple, yet profound wisdom changed our lives. This was not the first time Dr. Cole spoke life into our relationship, however. My wife, Rose, gained a new perspective on our marriage years before during a visit with him.

ROSE'S MEETING WITH DR. COLE

One of the fondest memories Rose had of Dr. Cole is when he invited her to join him for lunch in Dallas, Texas. I stayed up in the room while they headed down to the food court together. He offered to buy her lunch, but she wasn't hungry. He sat across the table from her with his cup of chili, and as was his custom, asked her to share her heart about everything weighing on her mind. He patiently listened as she explained her concerns about entering full time ministry and the current challenges in our marriage. The weight of ministry was straining our marriage and she was able to tell her "dad" all about it. It's necessary to have someone you and your spouse both agree can meet mediate between you and receive advice from.

He listened to her every word and then paused a moment, offering to buy her ice cream. When she declined, he offered her a bite of his own. It's not often that someone offers to let you eat off his or her spoon. The invitation made a statement that superseded the need to use words. Communication comes in three forms: word, gestures, and deeds. This is not a gesture a counselor makes to a friend; this is how a father relates to his daughter. She could confide in Dr. Cole because he loved her like his own family. Rose's heart was immediately softened towards him.

Trust became a common language the two of them shared. He then began asking her questions. *"Rose, do you love God?"* She explained that she did, of course, love God. After more listening, he asked her again, "So, do you love God?" She answered yes. Dr. Cole went on to say the words that changed my wife forever. He said, *"If you love God, then you have to love what he loves and hates what he hates. God hates divorce, because it's breaking a covenant and breaching what you committed to. God hates when we quit, whether it be a marriage or a ministry. He hates for us to only give our word and then break it. Rose, you can't quit!"*

At that point, something snapped inside of her. She realized marriage is not about honoring your spouse as much as it is about keeping your vow to God. When we weather the marital storms of life, it is a testimony of our love and commitment to God, something that can be inspired by others. Did you know that the word *integrity* was derived from the word *integrate*. Integrate is "to mold two separate entities into one." So, to have integrity is to be one with your word. We know God is one with His Word (John 1:10). He expects us to be the same. When He called out to Adam in the Garden of Eden saying, *"Adam, where are you?"* He knew where he was; he just did not recognize him.

Adam's lack of integrity and breach of character were unfamiliar to God. Man was made in God's image and likeness, but no He longer resembled his creator. When Adam sinned, humanity took on the enemy's traits and tendencies. God is holy – one, complete, never contradicting himself, and always keeping His Word. That's why the angels continually cry out, *"Holy, holy, holy is the Lord thy God" (Isaiah 6:3).* He is one with His Word; He cannot lie. God said it, it will surely come to pass!

God has asked us to, **"Be holy for, I am holy" (Peter 1:16).** We are to be just as committed to our word as He is! God hates divorce, broken promises, and failed commitments because they are the result of someone not keeping their word. When our actions do not lineup with our words, we are actually liars. Since God declares that all liars will have their place in the lake of fire **(Revelation 21:8),** we should strive to be holy!

Dr. Cole instilled in me that *our word is our bond* and that we are committed to keeping our word to God. There was an additional statement Dr. Cole made during his conversation with Rose that she did not share with me until several years later. Dr. Cole told her that I reminded him so much of himself during his younger years that it literally shocked him. He recognized the same drive that challenged his own marriage early on. He went on to describe how Nancy, his wife, handled this spiritual determination and focused lifestyle.

> *We are to be just as committed to our word as God is to His.*

Nancy had a unique way about her. She allowed him the freedom to be who God called him to be. God gave Dr. Cole spiritual ambition and momentum that took him around the world, and she was going to let him go. Nancy never gave him the *"ministry or me"* ultimatum, but instead supported his calling. It was something Dr. Cole loved about his wife. What greater gift can a woman give a man than liberty to be who God called him to be? There's nothing more attractive to man than a woman who supports her husband's God-given aspirations, calling, and purpose.

God gave many men that same drive and focus to pursue their calling, and they need not apologize for that. At the same time, we must recognize that anything out of balance, as with everything that stays in the flesh too long, becomes perverted. We must keep our supernatural work in balance with our family goals. Dr. Cole instilled in me that *balance is the key to life,* and he was right.

Spiritual fathers give great advice, because they've been through the hard times and have overcome the setbacks we're now facing. We have someone in our life we feel hears from God, someone we respect and know will not take sides; we have a mediator to seek marital counsel from. However, when

What greater gift can a woman give a man than the liberty to be who God called them to be?

we have no one to run to with our challenges and differences, we are more likely to run away or make decisions based on emotion instead of wisdom. Knowing we will stand face-to-face with a man of God and give account for our actions has a way of keeping us on track when we might otherwise get off course. The following testimony is from the wife of one of my mentored men:

> *One of the greatest benefits that I have seen with the mentoring program is that it makes men accountable for their actions on a consistent basis! Most people try to do something for a while, but give up when they're challenged. Mentoring teaches men that they must be men of their word and keep their commitments.*

We all desperately need a fatherly figure in our life that will charge us to give *account* for our *ability* to adhere to the word of God, thus providing *accountability*. It was not uncommon for Dr. Cole to begin his conversations with me by saying, *"G.F., how's your wife? Are you treating Rose right?"* It was also not uncommon for my wife to say, *"If you don't watch it, I'm going to call Dr. Cole!"* I knew in a matter of seconds that she could have him on the line; that, my friend, is accountability! It was good for me. It helped me to stay balanced while I accomplish my goals. Rose never actually had to call Dr. Cole in those instances because the mere thought of her dialing his number was always enough to make me reevaluate the situation and deal with it accordingly.

MARRIAGE- GOD'S ILLUSTRATION SERMON

I used to think God instituted marriage so we would not be lonely, and we could have children. I since learned that marriage actually serves a much more eternally significant purpose. It's an illustrated sermon in our life, a constant example we can use to learn about our covenant with God.

When God told Adam in the Garden of Eden, "**It's not good for man to be alone**" **(Genesis 2:18)**, I don't believe it's because Adam was lonely. He had a close, face-to-face relationship with his Creator, which was bound to satisfy his need for companionship. (**"Psalm 16:11, "In thy presence is the fullness of joy"**.) I believe what God was saying is, "It's not good for man to be **all-one**." As long as Adam possessed all he needed within himself, how would he ever know what it means to depend on God? How would he understand God's jealousy for him and God's desire for his affections? How would Adam understand covenant?

In marriage, a man is to become one flesh with his wife (Ephesians 5:31). This is God's way of illustrating our "one-ness" with him – "**That they all may be one; as now, father (art) in me, and I in thee, that they also may be one in us: that the world may believe that thou hast sent me**" **(John 17:21)**.

Through marriage, we understand what it means to forsake all others and commit to one person, just like God wants us to serve him and him alone – "**with their idols they have committed adultery**" **(Ezra 23:87)**. We learn about Jesus' relationship to the church through a man's love for his wife – "**Husbands, love your wives, even as Christ loved the church, and gave himself for it**" **(Ephesians**

5:25). We learn how to follow Christ by observing a woman's submission to her husband – **"Therefore, as the church is subject to Christ, so let the wives be to their husbands in everything" (Ephesians 5:24).**

I realized that my inability to understand and relate to my wife was not understanding and relating to God. I came to understand that my marriage was much bigger than learning to live happily with Rose. My marriage was a tool God was using to increase my revelation of him. God's biblical pattern is to teach us spiritual truths through natural circumstances. We first grasp the natural and then we see the spiritual connection (**1 Corinthians 15:46**).

My inability to understand and relate to my wife was just an indication I was not understanding and relating to God.

Rose's growth into a loving supportive wife has radically impacted the way I now serve God. Her meek and quiet spirit speaks louder than words to me. Even though I am anatomically made to be a giver, my marriage to Rose has taught me how to receive – a revelation I had to have in order to move forward in Christ. And even though women are anatomically made to be receivers, they learn through marriage how to give, which is vital to their spiritual existence. As we strive to understand our mate, we actually gain revelation of the desires and nature of God.

SETTING THE EXAMPLE

When Eve gave into the enemy's temptation, Adam knew good and well what was going to happen – she was going to die. Adam was then forced to make a decision. He had to choose to follow God, the *gift giver*, or Eve, the *gift*. We all know what Adam elected to do. Eve's decision was based on deception, but Adam was motivated by pure defiance towards

God. He openly chose the creation over the creator.

God gave Adam three opportunities to repent, but he remained in hiding and even tried to blame God! There's a big difference between Adam and Jesus. Adam died with his wife; Jesus died for his wife (the church). Adam took from the tree; Jesus died on the tree.

Adam died with his wife; Jesus died for His wife (the Church).

According to **Ephesians 5:23**, God has called me, the man, to be the savior of my family and to die to myself so that my wife and children can live. I realized the practical application of the Scripture some years ago when I went to God in prayer about my children. I have three boys, and as you can imagine, their behavior can be challenging at times. I was surprised to hear God's response to my plea that he change my children – *"G.F., you're the head of your family. If you want your children to change, you have to change first."* Yet again, God's wisdom worked in my life. I found that the better example of Christlikeness that I set, the better my boys responded and behaved.

On a few occasions I have found myself torn between the voice of God and the voice of my wife. Once in a while, God will give me a directive that I know will require sacrifice or change on my wife's part. I want to obey God, but also want to please my wife.

The truth is, our love for our spouse is never to be used as an excuse to disobey God. In **Genesis 3:17**, God tells Adam that he is under a curse for heeding the voice of his wife at the expense of the commandment of God. If we succumb to the will of our children or spouse, knowing it is not the will of our heavenly father, we invoke a curse on our life!

No matter how "unpopular" you may temporarily become at the dinner table, you must not compromise the direction and level God is calling you to. God will reward your obedience, and your family will enjoy the benefits of it.

Also, if you will consistently pray with your wife, she will see that your motive is simply to abide in the perfect will of God, and the Holy Spirit will speak to her and give her peace. A spiritual father is especially valuable in cases like this. If your wife is able to see your father as her father, he can help her understand God's design and desire for both of your lives.

Dr. Cole truly understood what it meant to **love his wife as Christ loves the church (Ephesians 5:25)**. A great deal of his ministry was spent urging men to cherish the woman God entrusted to his care. Dr. Cole's revelation of the uniqueness of the female soul liberated women all over the world as he preached to the masses. His messages were to men, but they were for women. He was so determined to teach men to honor their wives that he printed and circulated business cards with the following:

24 Ways to Say "I love you"

1. Listen to her.
2. Always laugh at her jokes.
3. Tell her truthfully that you can't wait to see her again.
4. Offer her a backrub without asking for one in return
5. Call her to say you were thinking about her.
6. Bring her a teddy bear and chicken soup when she is sick.
7. Write her a poem.
8. Bring her flowers for no reason.
9. Send her a hand written letter to say hello.
10. Always remember anniversaries; bring her something sweet.
11. Kiss her in the middle of a sentence.
12. Take her on a long walk at sunset, and stay to look at the stars.

13. Tell her something about yourself that no one else knows.
14. Remind her that you still think she's beautiful.
15. Take a bubble bath together.
16. Watch a "girl" movie together.
17. Surprise her with a candlelight dinner.
18. Never stop trying to impress her.
19. Never forget how much she means to you.
20. Give her great big hugs for no reason.
21. Kiss her for fun- lots and lots; no other agenda.
22. Tell her you love her.
23. Show her you love her.
24. Tell others you love her- you are committed to what you confess.

God, I miss Dr. Cole!

Dr. Cole and Nancy with Rose and I in their home in Dallas, Texas celebrating their wedding anniversary.

11

ACID TEST

**"You can give without loving, but you can
never love without giving."**

After Dr. Cole's meeting with my wife in Dallas, I went
down to the lobby to help him load up his things and
head home. As I walked him to his car, I can remember
thinking, *"Dr. Cole has blessed my life tremendously. How
can I bless him?"* About that time he arrived at his vehicle
and I was surprised at what I saw. His car was an older model,
not at all what I expected. It was in decent condition, but it
just did not seem to fit "my hero". It was at that moment that
I decided somehow, someway, I would make sure he had
a brand new, top-of-the-line vehicle. A material gift could
never compensate for the spiritual impartations he brought
my life, but it would serve as a token of my appreciation.
I was not looking for accolades or endorsements from Dr.
Cole; I simply wanted to honor him with a gift that would
speak volumes.

When you seek to give a gift of that magnitude, you
always have a "Judas" claiming there is a better use for
"such precious oil," but Jesus rebuked that attitude. Jesus
said he was touched by the woman's decision to break her
valuable alabaster box and honor him while he was still

around to do so. He went on to say that as long as the Gospel was preached, the account of her selfless act would be told (**Mark 14:3-9**).

I also realized that every time Dr. Cole would drive his new vehicle, he would have to think of Houston and Katy, Texas. Since I covet his prayers, I knew we would get at least one thought a day!

We were preparing to host a Houston Men's Event at our church in a little over a year, and Dr. Cole was going to be our premier speaker. I knew that would be the ideal time to bless Dr. Cole with the car. A man of his stature should travel in God's best, which brought me to the conclusion that he needed a new Lexus SUV! I shared the goal with other local pastors and they rallied to the cause. We saved up, gave into the purchase, and we were able to buy Dr. Cole that brand-new Lexus SUV. One of the greatest moments in my life was when we handed him the keys at the conference.

THE EVENT I'LL NEVER FORGET

It was February of 2000 and our sanctuary looked like an ocean of men! Our seating accommodated 1,000 at the time, so you can imagine what happened when 2,000 men entered our building to hear Dr. Cole minister at "Breakout 2000." They filled the gaps between the chairs and walls, stood in the very back of the room, and even sat by the choir on the stage. When we could no longer fit another person in the sanctuary, we escorted an additional 500 men up to our youth facility for overflow seating where they watched Dr. Cole on the big screens. Amazing! There was no football game, car show, fishing Expo, or boxing match at our church and yet hundreds of men spent their Saturday with us. The truth is, while he may not express verbally, every man hungers and yearns to know what being a man is all about.

"Breakout 2000" was a celebration in recognition of

50 years of ministry for Dr. Cole and the Christian Men's Network. Approximately 45 pastors came and brought their men to honor the occasion. We had been working for months to make sure this event lived up to its potential. All the men I mentor took an active role in gaining support from local pastors and communicating the vision and significance of the conference.

We not only had 2,000 men attend that day, but we also fed all of them lunch in a record amount of time! My mentored men and the men they mentor organized and executed an efficient game plan that allowed every man to enjoy a hot plate of Texas BBQ in just 30 minutes. I was able to greet the people and attend to Dr. Cole because the PowerHouse men and their wives were handling everything like true experts. As a pastor, that is a very refreshing and reassuring achievement. It also speaks volumes about the creativity and capabilities men have if we just offer them a challenge and allow them to utilize their God-given gifts.

As always, Dr. Cole's message provoked men of all ages, races, and walks of life to turn from sin and embrace Godly manhood. The altars were full and testimonies of dramatic life changes flowed in for months after the event.

As the meeting came to a close, it was time to give Dr. Cole his gift. I advised the pastors to come on stage with me because this present was from all of us. I held a small black box in my hand as I briefly spoke of our appreciation and gratitude for the labor of love he had so selflessly sewn into the life of men all over the world. For half a century, he had served as a missionary to men, and, like many of the pastors on stage, I was a directed beneficiary of his life and leadership.

The moment finally arrived and I held up the box. Dr. Cole looked quite puzzled as I began to open it. His expression became more perplexed when he saw what was inside. A single black key with the golden "L" was placed in his hand. His eyes lit up when he realized it was a car key, but he was altogether shocked when I told him it belonged to a brand-new Lexus SUV! He gasped, burst into laughter, and then started to weep. The atmosphere was electrifying as 2,000 men stood to their feet and applauded the delight they saw on Dr. Cole's face. Some shouted, others whistled, and some cried as Dr. Cole leaned forward to brace himself on his knees, still in awe of the moment.

Mission accomplished – my hero was truly touched. He gave me a loving hug and then made his way around the stage, hugging and thanking the other pastors. The car meant a great deal to him, but what brought him to tears was the thought of men coming together and giving their finances in a unified effort to honor him.

We left the stage and walked through two solid lines of cheering all the way to the front doors of the church. It just so happened to be a crisp, cool, and blue-skied day, and there, in the sparkling sun, was his new car wrapped in the huge red bow! He asked me to drive him around in it because he had never been behind the wheel of such a luxury vehicle before.

Dr. Cole always said, *"You can give without loving, but you cannot love without giving."* That gift was an expression of the love that I, along with many others, have for him. I was later told that he appreciated the vehicle in more ways than one. His wife, Nancy, had passed away not long before, and he had been driving her car. The familiar memories were difficult for him to face each day. His new car represented a new season in his life. God had new adventures and a bright future in store for Dr. Cole. We gave him an off-road vehicle to symbolically say, ***"Go climb your summit!"***

OUR FINANCES, OUR LIVES

Our finances represent our life because they represent our time, which earns money. If the amount of money I sow into an offering equates to an entire days worth of work,

I've just given one day of my life that I can never get back. **When we sow finances of our own free will, we are in essence giving our life.** Most men find worth in their career. It is an entirely new level to gain worth and value by supporting our spiritual father.

> *When we sow finances of our own free will, we are in essence giving our life.*

From a logical standpoint, and also Biblical, this kind of giving makes sense. Just as a farmer understands that the soil quality determines the harvest quality, when we sow into a man of abundant character, success, and value, our harvest will be abundant as well. It also behooves the son to keep his father free of financial concerns so he can spend more time with God gaining revelations that will ultimately benefit the son. In addition, when a father is unencumbered by financial obligations, he can open up his schedule to meet the needs of his sons.

MY STOREHOUSE

"For God so loved the world that he gave..." (John 3:16). Giving is as natural as breathing when it's motivated by love. That's not to say that it's easy. Giving always requires sacrifice on our part. It's just that love has a way of compelling us to override our selfish tendencies for the greater good of someone else.

Our decision to give or not to give becomes the "acid test" of our heart. Just as giving comes naturally to the man who loves, taking comes naturally to a man driven by lust. *"Lust desires to please itself at others expense, while love desires to please others at its own expense."* That's why God says in *2 Corinthians 9:7* that He loves a cheerful giver. That word cheerful actually means hysterical, uncontrollable joy, and laughter. A person who cheerfully places their tithe in the offering plate, is a person who loves God, and their love is what God is after!

I think we can all agree that the most commonly used scripture reference for offering messages is *Malachi 3:10*. God makes it abundantly clear in that verse that we're to bring our tithes into the storehouse and provide for His house. After studying and teaching this passage numerous times, I found myself revisiting it yet again, and this time I was stuck on the word "storehouse."

Our decision to give or not to give becomes the "acid test" of our own heart.

I had asked myself, "What is the storehouse?" **I concluded that a storehouse is the place we go to when our own supply has run out and when we're in need of additional help.**

Before I became a senior pastor, the church I was a member of was my storehouse. That's where I was spiritually fed; however, as a pastor of my own church, I no longer came to the church to get fed, but rather to feed the sheep. In all actuality Dr. Cole was the one feeding me. He was where I went when I was dry and could not seem to hear from God in certain situations. He was the one with the experience and anointing I needed. *He* was my storehouse.

That revelation gave me clear direction on what the Lord would have me do. From that day forward, I gave the tithe into Dr. Cole. We continued to sow offerings into the ministerial efforts at PowerHouse, but our first fruits always went to the storehouse.

Over the years I have had many men read this book, hear me teach Dr.Cole's truths, receive many years of fathering, and yet very few men have taken the action to sow like this into our lives. The men have done greater things than we have because they imbibed our spirit. For Dr. Cole to say that no one had even given to him at this level shocked me. He had blessed many multi-millionaires, statesmen, and professional athletes all who were much wealthier than our church.

It is a hard subject to teach even sons because it sounds self-serving. It sounds like the father is asking the son to pay him a fee while no real father even desires the son to support him, but he wants to support the son for life. This is where the paradigm shifts however. If the son never sees himself as a champion of the fathers care, he remains an immature taker all the days of his life. An immature son is a huge disappointment to the father and can do nothing but reproduce immaturity in his lineage.

Pastor Larry Stockstill became my covering 2 years after Dr. Cole went to heaven. I tithe into his life personally, because he keeps me accountable; he fills my storehouse. Pastor Larry and his wife, Melanie, have been a huge blessing in my life, marriage, and ministry. I hope he lives forever!

GOD'S PERSPECTIVE ON GIVING

Even though tithing and offering requires our money, it's actually much bigger than earthly currency. Sowing our finances signifies our covenant with both God and man, and covenant is an eternal commodity. A wedding ring valued at $2,000 is worth far more than that to the bride who wears it. No amount of money could persuade her to sell it, because it represents her covenant with her husband. Likewise sowing our finances is much more valuable to God than the actual money we give. Our offering is an outward expression of our covenant with him; that is what means the most to God. Think of it like this, when you give to God, you are saying, "This is what I think you are worth." It is just as a man portrays the worth of his bride when he presents her with an engagement ring.

As a pastor, it is very reassuring to have tithers in the church, but it goes beyond financial security. What blesses the pastor is knowing that there are men and women who support and believe in the God-given vision of the church! Their consistent giving is encouraging to him because it is the evidence that they consider church membership a covenant relationship.

Our finances are one way we can make our appreciation tangible.

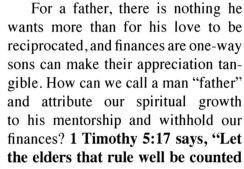

For a father, there is nothing he wants more than for his love to be reciprocated, and finances are one-way sons can make their appreciation tangible. How can we call a man "father" and attribute our spiritual growth to his mentorship and withhold our finances? **1 Timothy 5:17 says, "Let the elders that rule well be counted worthy of double honor, especially they labor in the word and doctrine."** We honor our fathers in the faith by placing value on their ministry through our time, talent, and treasure.

Malachi 1:6 says, "If I am your father, where is my honor?" That chapter goes on to say in verse eight that it is evil to offer blind and lame offerings. When we give less than sufficient offerings, we reap less than sufficient harvest. Many men would like to receive the wisdom and mantle of a man like Dr. Ed Cole, but few people want to pay the price he did to get it. He gave his sons his best so we must give our best. We are not just giving in to the man; we are giving into God's system for supernatural increase!

If were always on the receiving end, we're operating in lust; however, when we find ourselves searching for ways to be a blessing to the man that first blesses us, we know we're motivated by love. Loving our father back is really what it's all about.

I'm reminded of the story Mark Hanby told some years ago. He said his father was growing older and could no longer manage to live on his own. Mark discussed his father's condition with a doctor who informed him that his insurance would not adequately cover his long-term assisted living expenses. Consequently, they could not provide the kind of care he needed and they had no choice but to release him from the hospital. As Mark considered his father's newfound vulnerability, something rose up inside of him. He looked right at the doctor and told him, *"My father, who raised, nurtured, and admonished me, has something far greater than an insurance policy; he has a son to take care of him."*

As long as our father is alive, it is our responsibility to tend to his needs. As we sow seeds of time, talent, and treasure, we will reap sons of our own who will, in turn care for us someday. Let's do the right thing! Let's honor the ones we call father!

I want to close this chapter with the letter Dr. Cole personally sent me shortly after returning home in his new SUV. I have also included some pictures of the event.

> Dear G. F.,
> Sincere Christian greetings!
>
> I regret the delay for finally getting this letter done, but the car is an ever-present help in a time of need. I'm writing today to say thank you for your contribution to the purchase of the new Lexus SUV, which was given to me at our men's event at PowerHouse in Katy, Texas on February 3, 2001.
>
> It was a shock. It was stunning. It was totally unexpected. I don't know when in my life I was ever speechless in wanting to say thank you, but not being able to express it adequately. I still feel that way. God gave me something through you so good and great that it's hard to say a simple "thank you"; however, that's exactly the reason for this letter, to express my gratitude and appreciation for the largeness of your gift.

I pray that God will bless and prosper you abundantly because of your love for the Lord Jesus Christ and for what you have done to bless His minister. I'm still awed when I get into the car to drive. I'm very conscious that it is a gift from God through you and every time I sit in that car I pray God's blessing upon you and that he would prosper you and all you do.

Please accept this letter with it's inadequate expression of gratitude as being the best that I can offer at this time. In my whole life I've never had such a gift given to me. It is in many ways the greatest thing that has ever happened to me.

Thank you, bless you, God prosper you, and may his grace and favor continue to rest upon you as never before.

Yours in Christ,
Dr. Edwin Louis Cole

God, I sure do miss Dad.

(If this type of relationship appeals to you, then go get it. If you want what I have, simply do what I did. God is no respecter of persons!) –GFW

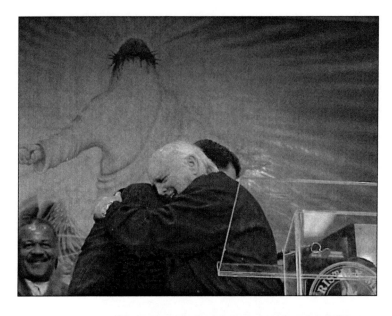

12

GOD GIVEN STRATEGY

~~

"Man wants victory, God gives strategy."

We began PowerHouse Church in a blaze of glory on June 16, 1996. Somewhere along the way, however, we lost ourselves doing "church stuff." We tried to do everything we'd seen work elsewhere to bring more people into our church, but in doing so, we drifted away from our deeper purpose and ultimate calling. We were busy trying to entertain people and meet their desires, but all the while, I was feeling less and less fulfilled as a pastor. I concluded that with the limited time we had on earth as human beings, we must aggressively uncover exactly what were called to do within the body of Christ to help God win His man back and do it with all of our might. Like Miles Monroe said, *"Purpose identified creates passion."*

Several years after the establishment of PowerHouse Church, I realized I had lost sight of my original drive and first love. It was Dr. Cole's truths and the concept of restoring men and reconciling families, that propelled me to start pastoring in the first place. So, I began researching and revisiting the revelations of *Maximized Manhood* and began again to teach men to love their wives, nurture their children, and function as a priest in their home.

About that time, I took an inventory of our group structure and faced the uncomfortable reality that the program
was floundering and failing to produce the "fruit" we desired.
My wife and I took the kids on a vacation to Hawaii. I was
in need of more than relaxation. I was searching for answers.

I brought and studied Joel Comisky's book on G-12
cell groups. Comisky compares and contrasts several of
the most successful G-12 models in the world. G – 12 is
based on Jesus's very own approach to ministry – disciple
12 men and empower them to do the same until the Gospel
is preached around the world.

While I was always big on delegating, administrating,
and equipping others to win the lost, I wasn't confident the
system we had in place at our church was the most effective. Our leaders are getting burned out as the result of the
constant cycle – make converts, nurture them to maturity,
establish them as leaders, and start all over with brand-new
converts. In the natural cycle of life, we raise our children
and enjoy watching them raise children of their own; however, our leaders were not experiencing the benefits of long-
term relationships that continually mature. Instead, they
were stuck with "diapers and midnight feedings." As our
leaders invested in building relationships, only to break off
and start all over again with brand-new families, the less
fulfilled and motivated they became.

After returning home from vacation the only answer I
had was that a change was needed, but I was not sure what
direction to take. Just days later I attended a Lion's Roar
Conference, hosted by Dr. Cole in Dallas, Tx. I was sitting
in the Board of Governors meeting with my notepad and
pencil when Dr. Cole unveiled his most exciting ministry
tool yet – curriculum that corresponded with all nine of his
books! Pastor Kong Hee, from Singapore, was there to testify about the great results he had personally experienced
with the curriculum at his church. Even though his church is

in Singapore, Dr. Cole's message successfully crossed the cultural barriers. Pastor Kong's 10,000-member church loved Dr. Cole's books and curriculum!

At that very moment a plan began forming in my spirit and mind, eventually developing into the MANCHURCH Strategy. I began drafting the idea on a napkin. What if we combined the character forming truths of *Maximized Manhood* with a plan designed to win the world through the vehicle of the local church? In other words, we could go beyond cleaning men up and start sending men out to achieve the bigger picture – the Great Commission!

God's ministerial pattern to send the Gospel to every nation is discipleship.

God's ministerial pattern to send the Gospel to every nation was (and still is) discipleship, as seen in the life of Jesus. Since the local church is the vehicle that mobilizes believers and incubates discipleship, why not use Dr. Cole's curriculum in the local church setting to spiritually mature men and then give them this model as an outlet to reach the world?

The concept proved to be a revolutionary idea. Sometime later, Pastor Eddie Leo gave his account of the dramatic effect Dr. Cole's curriculum had on his men. Pastor Leo's church is in Indonesia and when he first came across Dr. Cole's curriculum, "Majoring In Men," he had approximately 900 cell groups up and running! *"My only problem,"* he explained *to Dr. Cole, "is the 'cancer cells' that keep popping up."* Periodically, a cell leader would rebel against the vision and direction of his church, negatively influencing a cell group to share in his defiance. Like a cancerous tumor, it spread confusion and dysfunction throughout the church body.

Pastor Leo realized that the only cure was to build a stable foundation of character and integrity in his leaders. He found Dr. Cole's curriculum to be the best inoculation against deception and spiritual "cancer cells." Applying

127

principles of the MANCHURCH strategy brought a much-needed healing to his church body.

On the flipside, what good is it to be a Godly man, full of honor and character, if we never do anything to advance God's Kingdom? A pure heart and stable healthy home are not the ultimate goal, but they are a mere byproduct of serving God in a foundation that makes ministry possible. A family that flows in love and unity is equipped to overcome the spiritual and natural challenges of an evangelistic lifestyle. Dr. Cole's discipleship did more than clean up my home; it prepared me for a life of ministry. That's what true discipleship always does.

As believers, were called to build the church, not just men's ministries. Men's ministries in and of themselves do not perpetuate other men's ministries; however, when we change the man, we change the family, when we change the family, we change the church, when we change the church, we change the city, state, country, and then the world. While a thriving men's ministry does strengthen the local church, it is not the end-all answer to win the world, though it definitely is a starting point.

Furthermore, para-church ministries serve a significant purpose within the body of Christ, but their efforts must somehow connect to and grow the local church or they will not produce fruit that remains **(John 15:16)**. Take electricity as an example. Electricity is powerful but of no value to you and me until it is channeled through an electric power cord that connects it to our home. Ministry can be powerful and still have little or no value if it does not connect to the local church, the house of God (The Powerhouse). Just as scientist's have spent years working to invent the "superconductor," a substance that will allow for the least amount of electricity to be lost as it travels from its power source to an outlet. As a pastor, a leader, I want to see the least amount of people lost from the Kingdom of God and the church as they travel from their salvation experience to discipleship (spiritual maturity). An effective spiritual conduit requires relationship, consistency, and accountability, all of which describe the local church.

Sitting on the Board of Governors meeting that day, I found the motivation and inspiration I needed to make a change in our cell structure. I wanted to utilize the men as the leaders of the cell groups because that's God's biblical pattern and order. I'm certainly not against women rising to the call of leadership; I just don't want to see men shrink away from their responsibilities and calling. I believe men need

Responsibility is choosing to "respond" with our ability.

to be restored to places of authority and accountability in the home, church, and community. According to **1 Corinthians 11:3**, its God's pattern, **"But I would have you know that the head of every man is Christ; and the head of the woman is the man; and the head of Christ is God."**

Dr. Cole once told me that my purpose as a pastor is really not to train up the women and children. According to the Bible, it is a man's job to mentor, nurture, and disciple his own family. He's the appointed shepherd in his home and God has charged him to lead his wife and children spiritually. Maturity defined is the acceptance of responsibility. *Responsibility* is choosing to *respond* with our *ability*.

While most men live their entire lives never having tapped into their full potential, God has called us to exert our abilities and change the world around us. We cannot ignore, justify, pacify, or run away from the things that challenge our manhood; we must respond! If we want to see men mature, we must teach them how to take responsibility and stewardship of what God has given them.

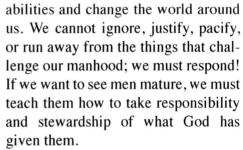

We cannot ignore, justify, pacify, or run away from the things that challenge our manhood.

I believe in empowering men to guide, guard, and govern their home; but what about the millions of single ladies who do not have a man to function as a priest in their home? We structured our church so that they have an adequate covering. Our Life Groups are designed to meet the spiritual, emotional, and practical needs of single women. Men in the group help with tire changes, home repairs, and the routine functions a male would normally provide. The women in the group extend a hand of support, counsel, and companionship. We even make arrangements like our father/son camping trips, for men to spend quality time with boys who do not have a relationship with their fathers. Our cell group leaders, as a couple, avail themselves to the single women who are a vital, active part of the ministry of PowerHouse church. Our single ladies preach, teach, and nurture the church body through many ministry outlets and have the benefit of mentored men protecting and covering him.

We have now defined and expanded the discipleship strategy which has revolutionized our Church. However, I almost missed it by settling for the "church as usual" mode of operation at the expense of my original calling and purpose. I think God that he reminded me of our covenant. Once again, I focus on Dr. Ed Cole's life, ministry, and message and sought out the simple, yet profound realities he brought to my life. I finally understood that my relationship with my spiritual father was not brought into my life just for me. Our relationship served as an example that I could base a ministerial pattern on, so that multitudes of men could experience the same benefits I had.

I stopped every effort, event, and ministry engagement that did not directly line up with the vision of restoring men and building the local church. I became, as pastor Rick Warren calls, "the purpose driven pastor" and entered a new level of fulfillment and satisfaction in my life.

ON YOUR MARK, GET SET, GO!

As a former athlete and coach, I have participated in numerous sporting competitions. For years it was my job to motivate young athletes to run faster, play harder, and push themselves to new physical levels. My continual search for new and innovative ways to energize and inspire the team always took me to the same conclusion – *victory* **is the best motivator that there is!** The scorching Texas sun, as hot and unforgiving as it is, is no match for young competitors whose hearts are set on winning. They'll endure grueling practices, constant correction, and physical pain as long as they know they're working towards a victory.

Victory is the best motivator there is!

When we have a trophy to fight for, we persevere. We overcome the urge to throw our helmet down and settle for the bench, because we want to stay in the game. We want to do our part. We also learned to put away differences with our teammates for the greater good of the team goal – **to win!**

What would happen at a track meet if as the athletes began to run, only to discover there was no finish line? How much effort would a football team put into a game if no one kept score? How hard would a baseball player swing if there were no bases to run to? How frustrating would it be to coach a team in a sport that had no winning objective?

How can the body of Christ fight the good fight of faith if there's no goal in sight, no way to measure up, and no structure for victory? As Christians, we also need motivation; victory is still the answer. Unfortunately, many churches do not have clearly defined goals or a game plan. Of those that have declared their mission, it is often vague and therefore never realized. For example, if a church goal states, "we will win our city," but there is no process or step-by-step plan in place to accomplish that goal, it will never happen. And when believers have no purpose or tangible goal to work for, they eventually find new outlets for their energy (often times it is spent bickering with teammates).

Matthew 24:14 is a "On your mark, get set, go" for believers. It says, **"This Gospel of the kingdom shall be preached in all the world for a witness unto all nations; and then shall come the end."** There is our finish line, our goal, and our prize! We're all grieved at the current condition of the world; the Bible tells us that famine, war, and chaos will only increase with time. Why not usher in the rule and reign of Christ? That's a real objective with a tangible, geographic goal that the body of Christ can achieve. I know God says we cannot know the hour in which he will return, but that doesn't mean we cannot pave the way. We can ensure the game doesn't go into overtime by following a winning team strategy.

Don't get me wrong – I'm not an escapist. I'm just trying to do what Jesus told us to do. I recently saw an interview with high-ranking military soldier and identified with what he had to say. He was asked why he was willing to risk his life in the war, Operation Iraqi Freedom, and if he was confident in our military strategy. His response was, *"Every decision we make is weighed against the end game strategy – winning the war. If we cannot prove a certain military action will ultimately bring us closer to ending this thing, we don't execute it. Make no mistakes about it, every step we're taking is leading us towards winning the war and saving lives. I'm confident in that."* The local church needs to adopt the same mindset; if our efforts do not somehow bring us closer to the rule and reign of Christ, why are we doing it?

Jesus initiated the plan to send the gospel around the world with his discipleship model. He portrayed the ultimate pattern of a father when he told his disciples, **"You will do the works I have done and greater"** (**John 14:12**). The true father is focused on the plan of God, not popularity. He delights in his son's success because it equates to the advancement of God's kingdom, and that is the motive behind his mentorship.

You and I cannot win the whole world by ourselves, but we can get one to get one to get one until the whole earth has heard **"The Truth!"** When individual believers see their worth and value in the overall big picture, they are motivated to press forward spiritually. The apostle Paul said it like this, **"I press toward the mark for the prize of the high calling of God in Christ Jesus" (Philippians 3:14).** What is our calling from on high? It is to reach the world with the gospel to end this game and bring back The King!

You and I cannot win the whole world by ourselves, but we can get one to get one until the whole earth has heard the truth!

Did you know if one person won one person to the Lord every day and taught them to do the same, all America would hear the gospel in just 28 days? If the gospel continued, everyone in the world would hear **"The Truth"** in just 34 days! Spiritual fathers are much more than a helping hand in times of need. They are a link to exponential evangelism and our conduit to reach the world. As we, the local church, embrace the structure that initiates and nurtures these relationships, we're following Jesus' very own example and we're working towards *Matthew 24:14.*

We're called to be fishers of men in the sea of humanity (Matthew 4:19). If we want our fishing nets to work, we must have a *network*! As we, the body of Christ, learn to link arms, open the lines of communication, and combine our efforts, we can see the Gospel preached in every nation. God tells us in Genesis 11:6 that when we unify around a common goal and strategy, nothing is impossible for us. I don't know about you, but I like the idea of being the generation that ushers in the rapture of the church!

I've already written a book called, "G – MEN: The Final Strategy" that breaks down all the dynamics of incorporating spiritual father /son relationships into the local church. The book you're reading now is about why we need spiritual fathers. When you combine the how with the why, it's an explosive combination! A pastor who caught both the message and mechanics of the strategy at the MANCHURCH Pastors Advance I hosted sent in the following testimony:

> *What made me fly from Europe to Katy, Texas for a week? Here are some important factors that I considered when deciding to attend the MANCHURCH Pastors Advance. I knew that these key areas had to be priorities of my church: growing through effective small groups, mentoring and being a mentor, reaching new souls, spiritually employing my men, developing leaders, retaining visitors, and getting outside of the box to be a cutting-edge, New Testament church in a modern-day world. All this was packaged in a strategy that I was not only taught at the advance, but through interacting with various levels*

of leadership at PowerHouse Church, I was also able to catch the DNA. This is working in Europe.

Reverend Desmond Frey
Pastor, PowerHaus Gemeinde
Luzern Switzerland

Man wants victory, but God gives strategy. The word apostle is actually a Roman word that means admiral or strategist. Prophets deliver a word from God and apostles implement it. Dr. Cole operated prophetically, while I tend to think and function apostolically. God is the mastermind behind these strategic relationships.

The body of Christ is ready for a game plan and God has clearly provided one. The concept of pouring your heart into other men may be familiar to you or extremely foreign, but nonetheless, it is God's strategy to end the game. While this form of discipleship may help your marriage, finances, and personal fulfillment in life, it's actually a building block in a much bigger plan – the final plan!

God, I miss Ed Cole!

13

ACCOUNTABILITY

"Mediocre men want authority without accountability."

There I was, on Dr. Cole's doorstep. His daughter, Joanne, and I had been communicating back and forth for weeks. She kept me informed of his physical condition. We both agreed it was time for me to make a trip out to see him. I brought one of my mentored men with me, and as we enter Dr. Cole's bedroom he was ready to greet us with hugs and affection, as was his custom. It was not easy for me to see my hero in bed, his stature now visibly affected by his declining health, but I wanted to be there with him.

Almost a year earlier, Dr. Cole slipped and fell on the ground, injuring his spine. His body had a negative reaction to the prescribed treatments and medication, which weakened his health; however, his physical challenges did not stop him from preaching the gospel. At almost 80 years of age, Dr. Cole was still traveling the globe. He was not one to complain about his pain, though I know he felt a great deal of it. I traveled with him several times during the final year of his ministry and I marveled at his ability to be a strong and courageous man in the midst of extreme physical discomfort. At dozens of conferences he had to sit in a chair while he ministered because he was too weak to stand for a lengthy amount of time. I remember seeing him lay flat on his back behind stage between sermons, visibly in tremendous pain, and then get out and preach for another 30 minutes. His body was weak, but his messages were stronger than ever. What a hero!

God had done multiple miracles to spare Dr. Cole's life. As an infant, he was diagnosed with a life-threatening disease. His mother took him to Angeles Temple where the infamous Aimee Semple McPherson was the pastor. When Pastor Aimee laid hands on Dr. Cole's tiny body, she prophesied that he would do great things for God. I think it's safe to say that she heard from God! Dr. Cole recovered from his illness shortly after and since that time, hundreds of people have received their miracle through his touch and prayer of faith.

Now he was resting at home and I wasn't sure what tomorrow would bring. It's one thing to feel you have work left to do on earth, but Dr. Cole had already made a lasting impression on humanity. He agreed with my vision to incorporate his teachings and curriculum into a strategy for the local church and considered it the next phase for C.M.N.; however, he knew he did not have to be here in order for it to happen. He'd already lived out his purpose. His two favorite people, Jesus and his wife, Nancy, were both in heaven, so I wondered how long he would strive to stay here.

I had a wonderful time with Dr. Cole that day. It was now my turn to extend a helping hand at supporting the man who had helped me on so many occasions. We told jokes, sang songs, loved on him, helped him walk around a little, and enjoyed just being in his company. I also spent some quality time alone with him, and the words he spoke to me in his significant last moments are forever written on my heart. I wish there was a way I could stay by his side, but we had to return home. We prayed for him and I hugged my hero goodbye.

A week later I received a phone call that Dr. Cole had gone to be with Jesus. His son, Paul, told me that he peacefully took his last breath and then drifted into eternity. I knew this was a glorious day for Dr. Cole, and I envisioned all of heaven giving him a standing ovation as he entered the gates; however, this was emotional and sad news for my wife and I. We knew this moment would inevitably come but somehow when it did, we were shocked. My father in the faith was no longer a phone call away. His belly laugh, soothing counsel, and reassuring hugs would only exist in my memory now. It was a painful realization and the void created by his absence only intensified as time went on.

As I grieved over Dr. Cole's passing, God comforted me with compelling revelations about this new season in my life. He took me to the twelfth chapter of Second Samuel, to the story of David and Bathsheba. To paraphrase, David fasted and prayed for his son's health to be restored, but the child did not recover. When David was faced with the reality of his son's death, **he got up from the ground, washed, put on lotions, and changed his clothes. Then he went into the house of the Lord and worshiped (2 Samuel 12:20).** This is not all he did. Verse 24 says, **"David comforted his wife Bathsheba and he went to her and lay with her. She gave birth to a son and they named him Solomon."**

God encouraged me to get up, worship Him, go embrace my church family, and focus on producing Solomon – spiritual sons that would someday build God's house! There was no time to waste. I was already actively mentoring men at that time, but God reaffirmed the direction we were headed. I believe with all my heart that was a prophetic word, not just for PowerHouse Church, but also for the body of Christ.

SERVANT VS SONSHIP

Dr. Cole's driving passion was *"building men and raising sons."* He continually held me accountable in that area. Even now that he was gone, there was no question in my mind that was what he wanted me to do with my life. Now that he was in eternity, he would no longer check my progress and follow-up with my commitment level. I wondered how many of the men that called Dr. Cole "father" would continue his life work of *"building men and raising sons."* About this time, God dropped another life-changing revelation on me: *"If you do the will of the father in the absence of the father, you are a true son."*

I thought of Jesus, crying out to God on the cross, **"Eloi, Eloi, lama sabachthani?" "My God, my God, why have you forsaken me? " (Matthew 27:46).** God was nowhere to be found when Jesus hung on the cross, yet He still did the will of his father anyway. He followed through with his commitment knowing God was not even looking at him. (Dr. Cole taught me that **personality is who we are when the lights are on; character is who we are when no one can see us**.)

If you do the will of the father in the absence of the father, you are a true son.

Confirmation of his friendship sounded throughout the land. The curtain of the temple was torn, the earth shook, rocks split, tombs broke open, and many who were dead came to life again. What's more, the people no longer cried out, *"If you are the son of God, save yourself!"* Instead, the centurion and all those who were guarding Jesus declared, *"Surely* **he was the Son of God!"** **(Matthew 27:54).** The words echo in my spirit once again, *"If you do the will of the father in the absence of the father, you are a true son."*

There's a big difference between a *servant* and a *son*. A servant works for a *wage;* a son works for an *inheritance*. A servant is *obligated* to work; a son is *motivated* to be about his father's business. A servant's work is done when his master is no longer alive, but a son's work is just beginning.

I know Jesus' love for you and me led Him to climb onto

the cross, but I truly believed it was His love for the father that kept Him up there. My love for God's people led me to the concept of the MANCHURCH Strategy, but my love for my spiritual father, Dr. Edwin Louis Cole, motivates me to keep telling the world to "build men and raise sons." It's God's strategy to "end the game."

DR. COLE'S HOMEGOING

Hundreds of men, along with their wives, filed into two lines and waited on either side of the street. Flags from 210 nations appeared above the crowd and the commanding sound of drums and bagpipes filled the air. It was an occasion fit for royalty.

A reverent hush fell over the assembly when, in the distance, we saw the gleaming white hearse making it's way towards us. As our hero passed by, men lowered their flags and silently feel in line behind the funeral procession. There was scarcely a dry eye as we approached the burial site. Some men wiped away their tears while others simply could not hold back the rush of emotion the moment evoked.

Dr. Cole requested that he be buried in a plain pine box. Paul had the C.M.N logo branded on the casket and Dr. Cole's infamous black hat, an akubra, was carefully placed on the top. I watched through tearful eyes as they lowered my hero into the ground. As I glanced around, I saw the look of sorrow on many faces. That was the amazing thing about Dr. Cole – he managed to touch so many lives in so many ways.

It is said of Samson that, **"He killed many more [of his enemies] when he died than when he lived"** (Judges 16:30). As Dr. Cole's body was placed in it's final resting place, my hope was that the same would be said of him. If his sons were willing to accept the accountability and responsibility of raising sons of their own, we could multiply Dr. Cole's efforts and execute a stronger battle plan against the enemy.

The home going service was held a week later at the Potter's House in Dallas, Texas. I, along with many others, shared heartfelt stories of the love and appreciation we felt for Dr. Cole. Some of the testimonies brought tears, others laughter, but one common thread united all of our experiences – Dr. Cole's influence had shaped our lives and built our houses!

As I listened to one story after another, I could not help but think, *"It's not what we say here today that matters, but it's what we do tomorrow that counts."* "Building men and raising sons" is the 21st century church model. Ed Cole saw it and began it; now we must do it! It's our job to ensure that this message does not stop at men's events, but becomes relevant and applicable to the local church. We must compel pastors to persevere beyond staunch religious beliefs and empty traditions so they can embrace the strategy and restore God's order to the church!

Like I mentioned before, I was given the honor of speaking at Dr. Cole's home going memorial service. As I shared what the Lord had placed on my heart, the greatest illustration I had to offer that day was not props, but people! I invited over 30 PowerHouse men to stand on stage with me. It meant a great deal to me that they all made the trip to Dallas, which spoke volumes of their personal gratitude for Dr. Cole's impact on their lives.

As they formed a straight line across the stage, we uniformly reached for our swords. We did not simply go out and purchase swords for this occasion. Each man diligently earned his sword by completing all nine of Dr. Cole's books and curriculum. Their accomplishment was previously honored at a commissioning ceremony where they received their sword, symbolizing their commitment to God.

When I gave the signal, we drew our swords in unison. With a stage full of maximized men holding their swords high, a long speech was not necessary. Thirty maximized men saluting their spiritual grandfather spoke louder than words.

REVERSING OF THE CURSE

Whether you knew Dr. Cole on a personal level, or never heard of him until you picked up this book, we all have an obligation to apply the principles he passionately preached (and practiced) to the body of Christ. It is more than a moving message and bigger than a men's movement; it is God's end-time strategy.

Malachi 4:5 says, "See, I will send you the prophet Elijah before that great and dreadful day of the Lord's coming. He will turn the hearts of the father to their children and the hearts of the children to their fathers; or else I will comment strike the land with the curse."

I don't think Dr. Cole was the prophet Elijah, but I do think he carried his mantle and message. I believe he was sent from God to turn the hearts of the fathers. After all, that was the heartbeat of his ministry. God makes it clear in this passage that we're to heed the warning and wisdom of the man of God or a curse will overtake our land. You don't have to be spiritual to look around our nation and see the signs of the curse. Look no further than our public high schools. It has been reported that approximately 2,700 high school girls get pregnant every day!

The plague of fatherlessness is increasing at an exponential rate and the Church must do something about it.

Close to half a million newborns will enter the world without a stable father figure every year! Since sexual immorality among teenagers is on the rise, so is that number. I met a man who had completed extreme research and discovered that in America, **over 6 million** women go to church without their husbands every Sunday!

The plague of fatherlessness is increasing at an exponential rate and the church must do something about it. God tells us in **James 1:27, "Pure religion and undefiled before God**

and the father is this, to visit the fatherless and widows in their affliction and to keep himself unspotted from the world." How can we be fathers to the world unless we first have fathers in the church? Before we can meet the needs of the fatherless society, we must be willing to become fathers ourselves. Like the old cliché says- **if were not part of the solution, we're part of the problem.**

I want to take a moment to point out that *mothers* are crucial in the church as well. While I ultimately hold the men in my church accountable to ensure their own lives, I also recognize the value a spiritual *mother* can have in a woman's life. Titus 2:4 says that the older (more spiritually mature) women are to train the younger women. My wife has availed herself to the women in our church in the same manner that I have the men. She is an invaluable part of the ministry and her gifts work in conjunction with mine to create a ministry team.

As we focus on our role as *fathers*, we cannot underestimate the importance of *mothers*. Both are necessary in God's house.

ACCOUNTABILITY- THE PRICE OF AUTHORITY

One glaring illustration of the need for spiritual fathers and accountability came shortly after I met Pastor Larry Stockstill. A prominent minister had committed sin and fallen from Grace. His congregation was over 14,000 members while his influence reached millions. His mistake was when he stepped out from under his spiritual covering. Here's what I saw: he, like many other men, became larger than the ministry that the Lord had given him. At some point submitting to a spiritual father became a secondary priority to him. No accountability leads to sin and destruction.

Rose and I were asked to be a part of a team that accompanied Pastor Larry Stockstill to conduct an Encounter God Weekend for the church staff. Over 100 men and 100 women staff were in attendance. These people were hurt, angry, broken, disengaged from church, pastors, and yes, some said they were even angry with God.

You see, when leaders do not submit, they will fall. When leaders fall, all those who follow them fall as well. This goes for President's, celebrities, sports figures, etc.. We all must be in an accountability relationship with a mentor/ father.

Dr. Cole said, *"Mediocre men want authority without accountability."* We must all ask ourselves, have I esteemed ministerial titles above ministry itself? Have I focused on getting into the limelight more than bringing people into the Lord's light? Has success become more important to me than significance? Father/son relationships do require accountability. So, we must all choose – do I want a life of mediocrity or Christlikeness? We cannot have both.

God, I miss Dr. Cole.

14

GREATNESS

_

"You do not measure the greatness of a man by his children, but by his grandchildren."

I like to wake up early on Sunday mornings and enjoy hot cappuccino at Starbucks before church. One particular Sunday, I took my son, Cole, with me. We pulled into the parking lot and realize we had arrived before Starbucks was open. I took out my Bible and figured I'd enjoy some quality time with my son. Just as our conversation was getting off the ground, I was startled by a loud knock on my window. It was a Starbucks employee who had two drinks in his hand.

I roll down the window and he handed me my Grande Carmel Macchiato. It was fixed just like I like it- extra, extra hot. He handed the other coffee to Cole and told us our drinks were on the house!

We were feeling extremely blessed as we finally headed into Starbucks. I was sipping on my coffee when the zealous employee approached us once again. "I'm really enjoying the _Maximized Manhood_ curriculum," he said. I suddenly realize this man was involved in our mentoring program. I asked him who his mentor was and he told me he was part of Mike Campbell's group. I congratulated him for investing in his spiritual growth and thanked him once again for the complimentary coffees.

As he walked away, I could not help but marvel about the fact that his mentor, Mike, was mentored by John, whom I mentor. It was an amazing thought – *I'm a grandfather!* It was a proud moment to realize one of my sons in the faith was effectively discipling his own sons. In essence, Dr. Cole's spiritual great-grandson just served me coffee! This experience, building men and raising sons generationally, was confirmation that the MANCHURCH Strategy was indeed serving its purpose.

> *Dr. Cole is in heaven, but his lifetime of ministry is still building God's Kingdom on earth.*

Dr. Cole is in heaven, but his lifetime of ministry is still building God's kingdom on earth. I wonder what that must be like, walking on streets of gold wearing a heavenly crown that keeps multiplying in jewels! Your work on earth is through, but your reward is still chasing you down. I wonder if that's what **Deuteronomy 28:2** means when it promises *blessings will overtake us* if we hearken to the voice of the Lord?

Experiences like that are what have led me to the conclusion that life is not a sprint, nor a marathon. Life is actually a relay race. We should be building on the progress of our fathers in the faith so we can pass on the baton of experience and achievements to our sons. They can then run faster and farther. As they springboard off of our accomplishments, and their sons launch off of theirs, the move of God goes from *glory to glory and faith to faith*! My job is to carry the torch in my generation and make the most of the piece of the puzzle I've been given.

PERVERSION VS PURPOSE

I pointed out in Chapter 1 that God's mandate to men

has not changed since the Garden of Eden, **"Be fruitful and multiply; fill the earth and subdue it...have dominion... over the earth" (Genesis 1:28).** God's strategy is to restore the dominion of the earth to His children. As a result, God put the desire in every man to be fruitful and multiply, but not every man knows what to do with that desire. When desires go unmet, dissatisfaction and unfulfillment sets in. Driven by frustration, we then search out unusual and often unnatural ways to become fulfilled.

When a man does not understand his God-given drive to reproduce spiritually, through discipleship, his inclination is to reproduce naturally, in the flesh. Disconnected from his divine purpose, perversion becomes his only natural outlet. The energy that was intended to fuel his spiritual drive is misdirected to his sex drive. A man who is preoccupied with pornography is simply a man who lacks revelation about his spiritual purpose. His need to affirm his manhood is not being met on a spiritual level, so instead of "subduing the earth," he seeks to conquer women.

Perversion is the devil's counterfeit for purpose and like all sin, it promises to please but only enslaves. There is no fulfillment in perversion because lust is insatiable. Dr. Cole often said that pornography is a substitute for prayer. Men will use images of physical intimacy to try and compensate for their lack of spiritual intimacy with God.

Perversion is the devil's counterfeit for purpose.

Not long ago the media was consumed by the accusations surfacing in the Catholic community. Every headline and news report seemed to center around sex scandals in the church. People were shocked by the stories, but I must admit, I was not. A man committed to the local church is just as susceptible to perversion as a man of the world if he hasn't tapped into his God-given purpose as a man. **Hosea 4:6 says, "My people [Christians] are destroyed for lack of knowledge."**

God gave each of us a spirit and that is the essence of who we are. When I reproduce spiritually by pouring truth into the men in my mentoring group, I get an inner satisfaction that is on a higher level than physical gratification. That's not to say that I do not crave the affection of my wife or that my desire for her isn't in any way replaced. It's just that when we understand and fulfill the spirit, it keeps our flesh in check. Dr. Cole said the reproductive process is the most fulfilling action a man performs, both spiritually and naturally. It's easy to overcome lusts of the flesh when we understand truths of the spirit. **Like Galatians 5:16 says, "Walk by the Spirit and you will not fulfill the lust of the flesh."**

BENEFITS OF MANCHURCH

Did you know that 18 of the 20 largest churches in the world are cell structured churches? There are multiple benefits to a MANCHURCH discipleship structure.

First of all, developing a core group of leaders takes a tremendous burden off the pastor. In the 18th chapter of Exodus, Jethro told Moses he could not possibly handle every situation and meet the needs of every person by himself. He needed to raise up leaders and delegate his responsibilities to trustworthy, competent men. As pastors, we need to apply Jethro's advice to our own ministry. I had to overcome the tendency to do everything myself even though the age-old saying challenged my decision – "If you want something done right you have to do it yourself!"

I like to use the visual illustration of a rake and a wheel to describe two types of leadership. A rake administration is where the pastor supports 100% of the weight of the ministry. His staff, the prongs, merely drags along behind him. They follow his instructions but exhibit no intrinsic drive, because they have never taken (or been given) ownership of the ministry. In a *wheel* administration, the pastor is the hub in the center of the wheel. He imparts a vision and the staff (the spokes) in turn helps support the wheel (the ministry). They are given the liberty to develop and add their gifts to help the wheel spins faster. Of course, Jesus is the **wheel in the middle of the wheel (Ezekiel 1:16)!** Wheel leadership brings self-fulfillment and advances the Kingdom of God at an accelerated rate.

2 Timothy 2:2 tells us to empower faithful men to teach others. As a boy, my father, Gayle Watkins, taught me a powerful concept he learned as a coach and principal in our Texas public schools. He told me that the best way to compensate for our weaknesses is to add people to our team who excel in the areas that we do not. Instead of feeling threatened by another man's strengths, we must learn to embrace and make use of his gifts. In the book *Good to Great*, Jim Collins points out that all great companies have CEOs that understand this principle; they call it *hiring to your weakness*.

Another benefit I've experienced since investing in spiritual sons is newfound flexibility on the rare occasion when I cannot be present to preach on a Sunday or Wednesday. I now have competent man who can minister in my place. I don't let just anyone step behind the pulpit, but I have spent quality time with these men and I'm perfectly at ease putting them in charge of the service. The mentored men enjoy the practice and are growing from the experience. Furthermore, the congregation always welcomes and supports them. They are like older sons, role models to younger siblings.

As a pastor, it's refreshing to know that when we happen to be away on a ministry trip or vacation, our church services will not suffer a bit. Dr. Cole taught that you're only a success we we you've trained up a successor – I am now reaping the rewards of that truth. The next benefit I've enjoyed as a result of spiritually fathering other men is open and honest communication about the ministry. Committed men are a great soundboard to bounce ideas off of, and they continually bring creative and innovative suggestions to the table. God has called the pastor to lead as a visionary, but the input and honest perspective of the mentored men is invaluable. Three separate scriptures in the Bible emphasized the need to have "a multitude of counselors" (**Proverbs 11:14**). **2 Chronicles 13:1** tells us King David consulted with his leaders who were given charge over the people. It's not uncommon for a shepherd to become unacquainted with the needs and issues of the sheep from time to time, but a mentoring group keeps the pastor informed and in touch with the flock. I have also seen the truth, **"iron sharpens iron" (Proverbs 27:17)** work in my men. They are iron-men.

Another significant benefit I've experienced with the MANCHURCH model is the ability to communicate vision. **Habakkuk 2:2 instructs us to, "Write the vision and make it plain so those who read it can run with it."** I know what it's like to strive to make the vision plain, only to discover that no one is reading it! The consistent quality time we spend with our mentoring group ensures that the vision God has given us not only enters their mind, but also their heart. Simply stated – they get it! They understand what we're trying to do with how we're doing it. Since they're all in the same group, they all come from the same seed, which creates great loyalty, unity, and purpose of vision. We use Dr. Cole's books and curriculum as the foundational "seed bed."

As my mentored men pour into their wives and discipled men, the vision is passed down exponentially. As a result there is an uncommon unity at our church. Unity is a powerful dynamic because where there is unity, God commands his blessings (**Psalm 133**).

The final benefit I'd like to mention is the one I have emphasized throughout this book. The mentored men are growing in Christ. Like a proud papa, I watch as each one of them increases in character and matures in their calling. Month after month and year after year, the anointing on their life intensifies and the blessing of the Lord becomes more evident. The genuine transformation I've seen in them means far more to me than any other ministerial accomplishment I can imagine.

The Bible says there is a friend that sticks closer than a brother (**Proverbs 18:24**) and that is the kind of relationship I desire to cultivate with the men I mentor. Discipleship relationships are for life. As God calls some of my guys to start works of their own, our relationship will only increase. They will go on to develop spiritual sons in other parts of the city, country, and world, thus providing a multitude of spiritual grandchildren.

12

I have found that the number 12 is very relevant and strategic in light of discipleship relationships. It is not feasible to think that we can maintain healthy close-knit father/son relationships with more than 12 people at a time. Even with a limit of 12 men in the mentoring group, it can be challenging to meet all their needs. We must also consider that our wife and children are our top priority and should come before our mentored men.

A twelve-man discipleship group is a long-term ultimate goal. Starting with a group of three to five men is probably a more realistic number. As those men grow older, stronger, and more spiritually mature, they require less oversight from you. That's when you can bring on a few more sons, but 12 is always a maximum lifetime number! If Jesus stopped at 12, so should we.

A VALUABLE LESSON

If you worked in the ministry for any amount of time, you've most likely seen the following scenario happen.

A man starts making subtle comments like, "*If I were the pastor, I would do this different.*" Over time, he becomes less restrained and begins openly saying, "*When I have my own church, I'm not going to do it like he does.*" Despite the many hours his pastor has been mentoring, training, grooming, and praying for him over the years, he's convinced he's "outgrown" his father's house. He's so focused on starting his own work that he gives little thought to training up a replacement to ensure that the ministry will not suffer in his absence. After confiding in several church members, he finally informs his pastor that he's leaving. He's not there to hear any concerns or "checks" his pastor may have his spirit about this new endeavor; he just wants him to know that Sunday will be his last day. He thanks his pastor for understanding and then ends the conversation with, "**By the way, the Smith's, Johnson's, and Jackson's are coming with me.**"

The body of Christ does many things right, but as a whole we're terrible at **transition**. Dr.Cole instilled to me that the way we exit one season of our life is how we will enter the next. If we leave our father's house in pride, offense, or rebellion, that becomes the foundation we build our ministry on. Consequently, we reap sons with that same spirit! According to **Galatians 6:7**, God is not mocked, whatever we sow, that's exactly what we will reap.

The way we exit one season of our life is how we enter the next.

I believe God sees church splits in the same light as divorce: he hates divorce because it is a breaking of covenant (**Mark 10:9**). When a ministry divides out of conflict, the congregation is forced to take sides, leaving them hurt and bitter. In time, their resentment turns into rebellion and before long, they cause a split of their own (or worse, they keep coming to church but continually bucking the system)!

When we take sheep unjustly from our father's flock, the

first fruits of our ministry are stolen! The tithe, or the first fruits of our ministry, is supposed to be holy and acceptable to the Lord, not dishonest and offensive. By stealing sheep, were acting like Cain – doing things out of a self-serving motive and then expecting God to bless it!

We were never meant to demand our inheritance and run away from our father's house. We should transition the right way: with integrity, honor, and the blessing of our father. We may very well be called to leave our father's house and start a work of our own, but we are never called to take advantage of or take for granted the man God used to prepare us. His ongoing mentorship will be a great source of strength as time goes on. Whatever we do, we must not burn that bridge.

God has called us to freedom, not independence. We're free to make our own decisions, but we were never created to depend solely on ourselves. We need the Spirit of God and we need our fathers.

THE FAMILY OF FAITH

God wants us to see our fellow church members as family. Paul wrote in **1 Timothy 3:14-15, "I am writing these things to you...[so] you will know how to live in the family of God. That family is the church"** *God has called us to freedom, not independence.*

(**NCV**). The local church is made up of our brothers and sisters in Christ and our mother and father in the Lord (our pastors). This may seem like foolishness to an unsaved man (**1 Corinthians 2:14**), but it is necessary in the life of the believer.

I am reminded of the time one of the men I mentor became deathly ill. He was in the hospital for four months, and on more than one occasion, the doctors took his wife into the hallway to warn her that he was not going to make it. Her days were spent running from work to the house to take care of her three boys and then back to the hospital to care for her husband. It was a physically and emotionally exhausting time, and she insists she would not have made it without the love and support of their cell group, her husband's mentored men, and the PowerHouse family.

This couple led a cell group and their group members made sure there were meals and transportation for the boys. They cleaned their house, walked their dogs, blessed them financially, and even replaced the refrigerator when it broke one morning. Above all, the church fasted and prayed for his miracle.

Each day that she arrived at the hospital, the waiting room was full of praying PowerHouse members. Their words of encouragement and faith kept her going. During those trying moments when discouragement would try to creep in on him, like clockwork, a church member would arrive at his bedside just in time to pray the prayer of faith with him.

As he lay in bed, in and out of consciousness, his thoughts were on his family. Everything inside of him was screaming to get up and go take care of his wife and boys, but he was too weak to lift his head on many occasions, much less get up. The anxiety of the moment may have gotten the best of him if it weren't for one specific memory that played over and over in his mind. He reflected on the time he and I made a covenant promise to one another several years before. We gave each other our word that no matter what the future held, we would always look after each other's family. He knew that no matter what happened, his wife and sons would be taken care of. That gave him a tremendous peace of mind in the midst of uncertainty and turmoil.

This man eventually recovered, much to the doctor's surprise. The love and support of the church family can literally be the difference between life and death.

GOD'S PERSPECTIVE

God has always viewed man from a generational perspective. It's not uncommon for God to break down a person's ancestral history before telling the account of their life. Have you ever found yourself skipping over all the "so and so begot so in so's…" throughout the Old Testament? God links the Old Testament Kings together by recounting one son on the throne after another. The Bible also clearly and carefully defined the genealogy

God has always viewed man from a generational perspective.

from Adam to Noah, from Noah to Abraham, and Abraham to Jesus. God even refers to himself as the God of Abraham, Isaac, and Jacob, the God of our fathers (**Genesis 3:15**).

Have you ever noticed that the Bible stops listing the long ancestral trails after Jesus's work at Calvary? Now that we live under a new and better covenant, we're no longer limited to our biological families. In **Matthew 12:46-50,** Jesus is speaking to a crowd when someone informs him, **"Your mother and brothers are standing outside, wanting to speak with you."** Pointing to his disciples, Jesus replied, **"Here are my mother and my brothers. For whoever does the will of my father in heaven is my brother and sister and mother."** You see, we have our blood relatives (biological) and when we have our other blood relatives (the family of God through Christ's blood)!

When God looks at a man, he sees his entire lineage, both natural and spiritual. According to Dr. Cole, raising godly sons is one thing, but Godly grandsons are the ultimate indication you've done your job as a father. If your son knows how to raise his sons, your mentorship was a success. You've created a legacy of significance that will continue far beyond your lifetime. In the words of Dr. Cole, *"Fame can come in a moment, but greatness comes with longevity."* **A**

good man leaves an inheritance for his children's children (Proverbs 13:22).

Long life is a blessing from the Lord. Ultimately, many of the elderly spend their final years in unfamiliar nursing homes, often abandoned; ironically, by the very people they gave life to – their children. However, with God's family strategy, we can grow older with the comfort of a huge family of men, women, and children who take responsibility for our well-being and quality of life. When taught correctly, a son will always take care of his parents. I thank Dr. Cole for the years he took care of my family and me. Without investment of time, talent, and treasure, my house would still be a mere blueprint.

God, I miss my father!

Dr. Cole with my son, Cole.

15

SONS

**"To be a good father, you must first learn
to be a good son."**

This is another one of Dr. Cole's chapters taken out of his book, "Absolute Answers." I believe it is a great entry as we draw near to the end of the book.

"To educate a man in mind and not in morals is to educate a menace to society," said President Teddy Roosevelt. One proof of that can be seen in the lives of some of the world's greatest philosophers of recent centuries. Those who were moral prodigals have done a great deal of damage to our world, and many of them had terrible relationships with their fathers.

Much of the inside in this chapter comes from Dr. Jess Moody, who made a study of the great philosophers. What he discovered is nothing less than astounding.

First, understand what philosophy is. It's a logical and critical study of the source and nature of human knowledge; a formal system of ideas based on such a study; and a basic theory about a particular subject or sphere of activity (Webster's new Collegiate Dictionary).

Philosophy is basic for living either individually or collectively. It under girds society. Every man has a philosophy by which he lives, no matter who, what, or where he is, how the philosophy was developed, or from whom it came.

According to Dr. Moody, there have been fifty-four great philosophers during the period covered from 645 B.C. until approximately 1960. Forty believed in God, and fourteen did not. Of the fourteen atheists, eight were preacher's sons.

Four of the atheists contributed mightily to the decline of the Western world. Of those four shared fourteen identical characteristics. They all:

1. hated their fathers
2. were heavily anti-feminine
3. were heavily anti-Christian
4. were heavily anti-Jewish
5. had severe psychosomatic illnesses
6. were repelled by human weakness
7. were weak in mathematics
8. had educational difficulties
9. were sickly in the last quarter of their lives
10. were depressive
11. had exaggerated fears
12. were extremely intolerant of opposition
13. made exaggerated claims that were not true
14. were suicidal

Three of these four were Darwin, Freud, and Nietsche, and each of these men wrote a book that influenced Hitler and Stalin. Those two men, in turn were responsible for the death of fifty-seven million people in forty years

Hitler hated his domineering father, a rabid atheist. Darwin's "survival of the fittest" doctrine was a great influence on Hitler, leading him to develop the philosophy of Aryan racial supremacy. Nietzsche's "Man and Superman"

and Freud's "Moses and Monotheism" also influenced Hitler.

Stalin hated his father as well. Dr. Moody reports that Stalin and his mother danced in the streets when his father died.

A chief characteristic of men who hate their fathers is that they usually adopt a surrogate father - someone to take the place of the despised. We find the same characteristic present today in young men who are "fatherless," who adopt a drug dealer or gang leader as a surrogate father. The dealers encourage and foster these relationships.

In Chicago, it was reported that gang leaders, drug dealers, and others "working the streets" buy the young boys shoes, jackets, gold chains, and give them money to further this substitute arrangement. Such an "adoption" process develops a strong bond and sets a pattern of behavior, as well as building a philosophy in the son's life.

Every son, through procreation, has a father figure in his life for proper maturation.

Fatherless men are searching for fathers today. Many times in my own life, as I travel and minister, men have told me, *"I never had a father, and through your books and tapes, you have become a father figure in my life."*

Every son, through procreation, has a father, but he must have a father figure in his life for a proper maturation. If his real dad isn't there, someone, somewhere, somehow will take his place. And, as in the cases of Hitler and Stalin, it often will not be a good substitute.

Something else occurs when sons hate their fathers: They tend to fail in school. Darwin did. It seems to be one of the ways they have of embarrassing their fathers, getting revenge for their rejection, or vindicating their anger. The high dropout rate in America's public schools today is probably directly related to the "fatherless" condition in the homes of so many kids.

Freud was a cocaine lover in the first third of his career.

He didn't believe it was addictive because the natives of South America used it for anesthesia when they were sick and for energy at work. When the news of his addiction was publicized, however, he lost his career.

I've always wondered how American became so addicted to drugs. Academia seemed to take to it, and the drug- using subculture of the baby boomers began on college campuses. When Freud's psychological approach to life was so rabidly endorsed and accepted in those institutions of "higher learning," it seems they also endorsed his trait of loving drugs and passed that along with his philosophy.

Today those same campuses are rife with anti-American philosophies, advanced by the same professors being paid by the country they dislike. How hypocritical! Decrying religion, denying God, the atheistic philosophy professor himself is a hypocrite.

Philosophy as a so-called science really can only ask questions; it can't provide any answers to the meaning of life. **"Claiming to be wise, they became fools," is the same way the scripture describes the unrighteous (Romans 1:22 AMP).** They changed the glory of God into something they made to fit their own image.

God created man in His image , and ever since, men have been trying to return the favor. What do you suppose the world would be like today if Darwin, Freud, and Nietzsche had enjoyed good relationships with their fathers?

Judge Bob Downing in Baton Rouge, Louisiana, stated that almost 95% of the young defendants who come before his court or who have been sent to prison from there admittedly hate their fathers:

> Crime is a male problem. In Louisiana, there are 19,500 men in prison and only 500 women, and some man generally got each of the women in trouble.

The problem does not come from the poverty, where they come from, or race – it's because they hate their father. They love their momma. Don't ever say anything about their momma or it's trouble. But the father was either not there, distant, or abusive.

I seldom see a young man in court who has a high school diploma, can name his pastor, and has a father at home who loves him

Young men from middle – or upper-middle-class homes come before me, and I listen to their dads wonder aloud, *"what happened?"* They think they have given their sons everything – food, money, clothes, cars, put him in the best schools, and played ball with him.

The mother will say yes, we gave him everything. I took care of them, made sure he was in Sunday school, and attended his sports events.

And after I heard this over and over again, I started asking fathers if they went to school or church with the family, and the answer is no. Dad stayed home and watch sports on TV, or went fishing or hunting. And, when the son got taller than mom, he said, *"If dad can find God on TV or in the fishing boat or out hunting, then I can too."* So, he's out the door.

Then he goes looking for a man he can look up to, and most of the time finds him in the wrong place. But the drug dealers and others know the sons need of a hero, buddy, or friend, they determine that it will be them.

We didn't have black-on-black crime years ago, when jobs were scarce and we didn't have running water. Why was that? Because Daddy was a deacon, Momma sang in the choir, and they were respected in the community.

Crack, the drug of choice, makes animals out of young men. Not even an animal though, would steal from its own parent. Crack addicts do. Railing against their grandparents for their Christian faith, pointing out their low-class status, faulting them for the lack of the "best things in life," they steal from them to support their habit, and then the grandparents mortgage that same home the grandson ridiculed to bail him out of jail.

Those grandparents may not have had much, but they had their self-respect and the respect of their community. They were looked up to. People had regard for them.

Nobody knows who invented crack, the most addictive drug in society. Al Capone wouldn't steal from his mother, and even a John Dillinger would not have taken his grandparents social security check, yet a "crackhead" has no compunction about doing anything necessary to support his habit.

Putting people in jail is not the answer. People look to government to solve their problems. Government doesn't have a clue how to solve the drug problem. It just throws more money at the problem in prisons and treatment centers.

Only Jesus is the answer. I see many crackheads saved, give their life to Jesus Christ, and be instantly healed of their addiction. It didn't take a 12-step or even a 30-day, $30,000 program to rehabilitate him. The government doesn't have to spend $35,000 a year to incarcerate him anymore.

When God restores a man to his family, he saves the whole family. The last words from the prophet Malachi in the Old Testament say that God will turn the hearts of the fathers to the children, and the children to the fathers. It does not say the mothers. Why? Because mothers take care of their children. It's only fathers who go off and leave their children. (Judge E Bob Downing, audiotape testimony, Baton Rouge men's event, Christian men's network.)

The son may stray from home, as I did, but he'll eventually come back as I did. Both my earthly father and my heavenly father welcomed me back.

That's the way it was with the prodigal in Christ's parable. Leaving his father's house, he eventually was living in a pigsty, (it could have been a crackhouse), and the pigs ate better than he did. He fed from pods while the pigs ate the peas. No substance to his diet – just husks. So it is with today's young men, brought into the world to reflect the glory of God, but instead living on husks, nothing substantial in their lives, and subject only to concrete authority because they have never matured.

The "finer things In life" that they hunger for are the virtues of real manhood – things that give dignity, worth, and value to a man. A man given to drugs is a fool. Here is what the book of Proverbs says concerning fools: **"The fool won't work and almost starves, but feels that it is better to be lazy and barely get by, than to work hard when, in the long run, it is all so futile"(Proverbs 26:11).**

To be a good father, you must first learn to be a good son. But if you haven't had a good father helping to bring you through the process of maturation into that maturity of manhood, you'll have difficulty in becoming a good father yourself.

Because my dad wasn't a good father, I lacked qualities of real fatherhood in raising my own children. Fortunately, because of my relationship with God through Jesus Christ, His Grace compensated for my lack, and my kids are great parents to their children.

My son, Paul for example, is the dad of a lifetime for his children. His philosophy of fathering was developed in a Godly home, where both parents love each other, the family prayed and played together, and friends of the family lent a positive influence to their upbringing. The philosophy of real Christianity will withstand the false ideologies and philosophies advocated in any school. Raised in the nurture and admonition of the Word of God, taught by the principles of righteousness, having a personal relationship with Jesus Christ, a son or daughter can withstand any onslaught of thought or doctrine.

Darwin, Freud, and Nietzsche, through their human philosophies, influenced Hitler and Stalin and brought to death and desolation to the world in their generation. The apostles Paul, Peter, and John through the philosophy of Jesus Christ, brought salvation, health, and life into the whole world.

Consider the results. Through Jesus Christ, believers are adopted into the family of God, and as good as sons of God, they are taught to be good earthly fathers.

Hatred of a father leads to rebellion and ruin.

My good friend John Binkley tells of the day when his blessings and prosperity began in earnest. It was while reading the Scriptures that the Word of God came alive to him, when he discovered that one of the Commandments came with a promise from God: if you honor your father and your mother, the promise is long life.

John's parents were retired and living on a retirement

income, and he had accepted their way of life without really thinking about it. After reading this principle, he began to study the condition of both his parents and the parents of his wife, Sharon. They both began to help support their parents, provide for them, hope to make sure they were well taken care of, with their needs met. Sometime later when he began to wonder why he was having such good success, he traced back to the time he made that decision. **God honors us when we honor his Word**. John's inadvertent negligence, when corrected, brought great favor and blessing.

Hatred of a father leads to rebellion and ruin. Repentance leads to reconciliation and restoration.

The hero of the parable is the Father, of course, who simply waited for the prodigal to grow up. We all have a heavenly father who, in great love for us, waits for us in our prodigal lifestyle to come to our senses and return to Him – to find again the inheritance we thought we had squandered.

Come on home.

16

THE MAGNIFICENT ADVENTURE

(This chapter has been added since the writing of this book 10 years ago.)

Without a doubt, our lives have been changed, elevated, and enhanced by accepting God's calling to build men and raise sons; however, we know that without a visible and audible model to follow, we wouldn't have had success. Following Dr. Ed Cole and allowing him to mold our lives also allowed him to view our willingness to submit to the patterns and principles that he believed in. He gained confidence by this process that we would reveal these truths to every audience we were exposed to. With confidence gained, Dr. Cole began to promote us by recommending our ministry.

His recommendations and endorsement opened doors for new adventures in the faith for us. A spiritual father that is convinced of the heart and head of his son should use his influence to open doors for him. The following list is composed of the adventures that our lives have been exposed to because of Dr. Ed Cole as well as Pastor Larry Stockstill.

- Took six trips to Africa to meet and minister to thousands. We enjoyed multiple safari adventures including exposure to elephants in the wild and lion feedings. I also took my family across the Namibian desert with dunes as high as a 4-story building.
- Planted PowerHouse Namibia with a foundation of restoring men.
- Ministered in Brisbane and Sydney Australia. We established the curriculum in Pastor Shaun Hansen's church where he has commissioned over 100 people in the last 6 years.
- Rode in Sydney Harbor by boat with Rose. She also trained for New York City Marathon by running around the Gold Coast as well as Sydney.
- Enjoyed Steve Erwin's zoo and actually handled Kangaroos and Koalas while exposing our Pastor friends, Tim and Chris Ennis, to this experience.
- Spoke in New Zealand and enjoyed staying at the Huka Lodge.
- Attended the New York City Marathon twice to support Rose.
- Supported Metro Ministries in Brooklyn by taking 28 volunteers to help them during their Christmas outreach. I have developed a strong relationship with Pastor Bill Wilson, who ministers to over 50,000 children a weekend at the time of this book.
- Attended the New York City Thanksgiving Day Parade- something my wife has always wanted to do. Cold is an understatement for that trip! I learned that when people really want to see or do something they will make it happen. Example, we walked two miles to get to a covering two hours before the parade would begin in 25 degree weather. Reports said that three million people lined the street. Here was my big observation: plenty of coffee and plenty

of donuts, but no bathrooms! No one cared! Don't tell me people can't get to church on time, sit in a climate-controlled environment, and hear great music and teaching if they really wanted to!

- Traveled on an Alaskan Cruise given to us by PowerHouse Church. Wow!

- Journeyed on a transatlantic cruise to Spain and Italy for our 26th Anniversary.

- Traveled to Hawaii several times and spoke for different ministers there. One that I fondly remember was an invitation to speak during Pro-Bowl week at an AG Men's Conference. We commissioned men who had been mentored by David Chang (a man I was blessed to mentor) and presented them with Samurai swords. And I attended the Pro-Bowl, oh yeah! While relaxing afterwards, I ran into Pro-Bowl hall of famer, Steve Young. We visited in Maui at the Grand Waialua, while our wives shopped. I found out that we played against each other while he was a freshman at BYU while I was at the AirForce academy. To me that was a kiss from God. Hawaii is one of our favorite places to relax. I am also petitioning the Lord to allow me to help govern one of the islands upon His return! Dr. James Morocco of the King's Cathedral in Maui and his family have become great friends. He was a friend of Dr. Ed Cole and is a friend of Pastor Larry. **Our father's friends should be our friends.** We have preached in Lanai, Kauai, Maui, and Oahu and loved every minute of it. We have been able to influence many of our spiritual sons and daughters to travel with us and meet our friends in Hawaii.

- We were able to minister in Lima, Peru many times as well as preach in Buenos Ares, Argentina. In 2011, we took 19 men to Lima and taught at the Focus on the Family, *Save the Family* conference. Having 19 men accompany me (one Pastor and three men from Africa) spoke volumes to the conference attendees. Of course, the topic was men.

- We left a spiritual son, Jose Lopez, his wife Kathryn, and their two sons in Lima to serve under the covering of Pastor Guillermo and Milagros Aguayo. Jose and Kathryn served for one year there and oversaw as many as five ministries for Pastor Guillermo. They then moved to Puira, Peru to plant PowerHouse Peru!

- We traveled to Scotland where we visited Pastor Bernie and Nan McLaughlin in 2003 and introduced them to the men's curriculum and commissioning. We returned in 2012 to realize that they had already commissioned over 50 men, and we commissioned 10 more. While there, we visited the William Wallace (from the movie *BraveHeart*) monument and viewed his actual battlefields and sword. We also were able to visit the home of John Knox.

- We visited London and viewed iconic landmarks: George Mueller's museum and Smith Wigglesworth's home, church, and grave. We also toured Big Ben and Buckingham Palace with my wife, sons, and mentor.

- I ministered at one of the largest spirit-filled churches in Paris, France. The church was about 90% female, and they took virtually all the product that we brought with us. They were hungry for their men to be men of God. While in Paris, we also visited Notre Dame and the Eiffel Tower.

- I married my oldest son, Cole, to his wife, Kelly. They met in the 8th grade at PowerHouse Church, and I am very proud that they both stayed sexually pure for each other and that their wedding day was a good one.

- I hosted Church Norris, Evander Holyfield, Mike

Barber, Charlie Ward (Heisman trophy winner), and Kirk Cameron at PowerHouse Church and Jordan Ranch.

• Lastly, I met Reinhard Bonnke and Pastor Yonggi Cho while with Pastor Larry Stockstill.

A RANCH FOR CHANGE

The men and women's Encounter God weekends impacted my life in a powerful way. For years, I had seen men and women come into the church, say a prayer of salvation, and then rarely see them again. If I did, I would not see much fruit in their lives to show that a transformation had really taken place. Then Pastor Larry Stockstill introduced us to the Encounter God Weekends. These 3-day Encounters are founded in His cross and your deliverance. We learned that while salvation can and does take place during a 2-hour church service, transformation normally needs a few intense days in the presence of His cross to take root and ultimately produce fruit.

We began to put hundreds of our members through these Encounters. We used retreat centers in the country to hotels in the city. After we influenced several churches in Texas to "come and see" these deliverance encounters, we were holding them every six weeks!

I believe it was at this point that the Lord spoke to me about building a retreat center that could fulfill several objectives of His church. Men, women, and youth Encounters could be held in an excellent atmosphere. Marriage retreats, leadership retreats, staff retreats, missionary and pastoral sabbaticals: the possibilities of events were endless! The difference was that this Ranch was designed to be one of a kind in quality, décor, and service. Originally the cost was set to be $2 million, but by the time it finished it was over $9 million. For so long the church has been a poverty-minded entity when it comes to retreats. God asked for us to build with His image in mind; there is nothing cheap about Him! We also wanted our ladies to enjoy a nice place to stay and not have to worry about the normal challenges of country camps. My wife, Rose, decorated the entire Ranch and didn't miss a detail. You should check out the website, www.JordanRanch.org, to see the beauty and rustic elegance of Jordan Ranch.

The ranch has been in operation for less than three years, but we have seen literally thousands of souls impacted for heaven. We also have been able to help people that we wouldn't have met if we only had a church and not a ranch. Here is a list of the people that have been impacted at Jordan Ranch: Wounded Warriors, Katy ISD, Schulenburg ISD, Flatonia ISD, Quilting Club, The Flippen Group, Boys & Girls Club, Marriage Ministries, and 50 other ministries.

METHODS FOR MEN

In an attempt to draw attention to our nation's need for Godly fathering, we began the **Intense Men's Gathering**. The event began in 2010 with 800 fathers and sons gathering at Jordan Ranch. We had several great speakers like Joe White, Bum Phillips, Mike Barber, Jack King, Bill Wilson, and Governor Rick Perry.

The concept of attracting men of all ages and cultures to eat, camp, compete athletically, and worship came from Africa. You may have heard of the movie "Faith like Potatoes", under the leading of Angus Buchan, stadiums were filling up with 40,000 to 50,000 men who camped outside between sessions. Texas and South Africa have a lot in common culturally and I felt led to host these father and son campouts and bring in speakers from around the world. Now, PowerHouse Church and the staff typically plan for about six months to prepare to serve the men at the gatherings. The theme for 2013 is "Armed and Dangerous" in support of our military heroes. We will be gathering with the Wounded Warriors to highlight the ways we can help our heroes.

In 2008, we began a website for men called *The Most Dangerous Game*. The theme is that men have the potential to do great things for society or to be a great danger to society. Men play with their eternal destiny on a daily basis like it was a game. If that is not bad enough, since men are the designated drivers of their families, they are either taking their families to heaven or hell based on their choices. This website has sections that deal with a man's marriage, money, and ministry. It is an attempt to be a mentor for a man until he finds his spiritual father.

The President's Club was designed as a part of the Most Dangerous Games, to give added touch and hopefully a degree of relationship for men seeking this. The benefits of the President's Club are conference calls, reserved seating at events we sponsor or outside events where I am a speaker, ability to bond with me at men's events, help in the commissioning process, free registration to the Intense men's event, consistent product mailings (CDs, DVDs, and books), and more. All proceeds received go directly to the Jordan Ranch project and the development of men and families. At this time there are over 1,000 subscribers to the Most Dangerous Games, 50 President's Club members, and 20 countries represented. We hope to build men and raise sons with this website.

APPRECIATION

The best is yet to come! I owe all of this magnificent adventure to the men who shaped my life: Gayle Watkins (Dad), Walter Hallam (Pastor), Ed Cole (Men's Minister), and Larry Stockstill (Pastor). Each man at different and critical points in my life instilled faith in me. Ultimately it was the Holy Spirit who was the guide that led me through each mountain and valley experience and gave me the faith to **"Take My Place!"**

17

PROVE IT!

"Change is not change until there's change."

H ave you ever heard the blunt saying, the road to hell is paved with good intentions?" As unrefined as that statement may sound, it's the truth. Many times we are guilty of meaning well, but never actually doing well. Discovering the need for change, and even desiring to change is not good enough. "Change is not change until there's change". We must act on our intentions because **"faith without works is dead" (James 2:26).**

Dr.Cole taught me that we tend to judge ourselves by our intention but we judge others by their actions. When a fellow co-worker clocks in late, we wonder why he can't "get it together" and show up on time. However, when we're running late it's because the traffic jam, faulty alarm clock, or some other variable beyond our control that we use to justify our actions. *It's not my fault; I meant to be here on time!*

In the twenty-fifth chapter of Matthew, Jesus tells the parable of the talents. Three men are entrusted with their master's talents and they each receive an amount proportionate to their abilities. When their master returns to check on status of his investment, there is no room for excuses, failed intentions, or self-justification. His servants now simply show him the physical evidence of their stewardship.

You see, based on the Scripture, faithfulness equates to increase. The man who increased was called good and faithful while the one who merely maintained was branded slothful and wicked. We must all ask ourselves – *what will my master call me for all of eternity?*

Two of the men doubled their talents, the one man did nothing with what was given to him. All attempts to explain and excuse why he only had one talent were immediately dismissed by his master. His single talent was given to a more faithful man and the wicked lazy steward was cast away.

In light of the previous chapters of this book, I want to charge you to move beyond intentions, and take a step of faith. Identify what excuses are hindering the discipleship process in your life and then make a change. If you have yet to search out spiritual father, today is your day for action. Remember we cannot become a successful father until we've become a submitted son- it's hard to lead where we've never been. Furthermore, if you have never begun the fathering process for others, don't hide your God-given talents; invest them so God's kingdom can increase!

In Matthew chapter five, Jesus uses simple parables to encourage us to be the light of the world and the salt of the earth. These passages may be elementary enough to use as nursery Sunday school lessons, but they also contain revelations that challenge men to the core of their being. If we have the light of Christ in our life, we cannot hide behind a bushel - or should I say a career, social insecurity, sport obsession, or hobby. Even the pulpit can be a place that men escape to, avoiding the vulnerability and accountability of relationships. We must be visible and apparent and approachable, a city set on a hill, for the men in our church, community, and sphere of influence.

We are also the salt of the earth. Salt is a preservative and so are we. If we don't labor to preserve our "ever rotting" society, who will? A mature man understands that the condition of the world around him may not be his *problem*, but it is his *responsibility* to provide solutions. When Cain asked God, **"Am I my brother's keeper?"** (**Genesis 4:9**) the answer is a resounding yes! And when Jesus said, **"It is finished" (John 19:30)** that was our cue that our mission to save our brothers (and sisters) was starting. God did his part now we must do ours.

I want to charge you with the simple question, one we find King Saul asking in the seventeenth chapter of I Samuel. David had just killed Goliath and Saul was amazed at the strength courage of such a young boy. His only question for David was, **"Whose son are you?" (1 Samuel 17:58)**.

Today I ask you the same question. You may be building a world changing ministry and doing mighty exploits for the kingdom of God but the question remains, *"whose son are you?"* Who spoke into your life and patiently groomed you until you became "giant slayer"? While some men seek to find their spiritual father, some of us already know who that man is; we just have yet to reach out and submit our life to his.

Then again, maybe you're like me. The man whose discipleship changed your life forever has gone to be with Jesus and you're now living out the life lessons he worked so diligently to instill in you. My question to you is, *whose father are you*? Where are your sons? Who are you teaching to rescue the lamb out of the lion's mouth and run at the enemy's camp?

I think one mistake we can easily make is to assume we have yet to run across someone with the potential to be a son. Maybe we're surrounded by men who are distressed, discontented, and dysfunctional. That was the exact scenario David found himself in the cave of Adullam, but it did not stop him from building an army. He used his influence as a leader to transform their depression into righteous aggression! They entered the cave of Adullam broke, busted, and disgusted, but staying close to a leader, a **father**, they came out mighty men of God. If a man's *heart* is right, your mentorship can help get his mind right. Once they've renewed their mind there's no end to what they can achieve.

There is a certain man in my mentoring group who I consider extremely faithful and dependable. He and his wife had been pillars of support in our church for several years now. He is an assistant pastor on staff at PowerHouse Church and almost all of our ministerial affairs are under his supervision in one way or another.

If a man's heart is right, your mentorship can get his mind right.

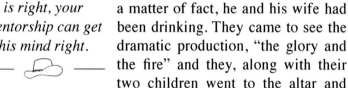

When he first came to our church, he did not come dressed in a suit. As a matter of fact, he and his wife had been drinking. They came to see the dramatic production, "the glory and the fire" and they, along with their two children went to the altar and gave their lives to Christ.

I saw them a few days later helping out at one of our neighborhood outreaches and from that day on, they became an active part of everything our church did. As my wife and I got to know them, they shared their remarkable testimony. At one time, he was a drug addict, living on the streets, searching for his next meal in garbage cans. His wife also had an equally powerful testimony. We spent time developing relationship and mentoring this couple, steadily working through their marital and spiritual issues.

If you can see this couple now, you would never guess they dealt with this kind of struggles that they did. Their mess became a message and their test, a testimony! It's amazing what can happen when we take the time to invest in people.

Another man I mentor, Pete Fajardo, sent me the following message testimony about his experiences mentoring:

I am finding that as I help men mature, I am actually maturing. I've also gained a unique perspective I did not have before. By taking on the role of a spiritual coach, and responding to the needs and actions of my men, I now understand my own needs and actions affect God. Becoming a spiritual father helped me relate to my heavenly father on a much greater level.

THE NEED FOR LABORERS

"And Jesus went about all the cities and villages, teaching in their synagogues, and preaching the Gospel of the kingdom, and healing every sickness and every disease among the people. But when he saw the multitudes he was moved with compassion on them, because they fainted, and were scattered abroad, as sheep having no Shepherd. Then saith he unto his disciples, "the harvest truly is plenteous but the laborers are few; pray ye therefore the Lord of the harvest, that he will send will send laborers into his harvest." (Matthew 9:35-38)

When people are healed and delivered in our church services, we shout for joy! We praise God and leave church feeling victorious. So why is it that after Jesus preached, talk and healed the people, he was sad? He was grieved because he knew that without a shepherd, organizer, servant, or laborer, the people would just go right back into the very thing from which he'd just released them!

The people Jesus ministered to her fainting because they didn't have a pastor, a mentor, or a leader. They fainted then and they're still fainting today. God is looking for men and women who are willing to become laborers in this hour – people who are willing to spiritually nurture someone to maturity. If you are a pastor, I want to especially plead with you to take men under your wing and begin fathering them in the word. Start with a few. All that really matters is that

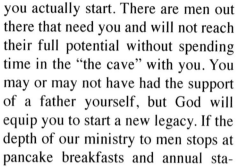

The depth of our ministry to men cannot stop at pancake breakfasts and annual stadium rallies.

you actually start. There are men out there that need you and will not reach their full potential without spending time in the "the cave" with you. You may or may not have had the support of a father yourself, but God will equip you to start a new legacy. If the depth of our ministry to men stops at pancake breakfasts and annual sta-dium rallies, we'll never develop the level of relationships that revolutionize a man's spiritual existence.

MANY NEEDS, ONE SOLUTION

As we focus on fathering, you may wonder what becomes of the needs of women and children. The truth is as long as we strive to mend what hurts the women and children, only to send them home to a broke, busted, and disgusted head (man), our efforts do not bring the permanent results we're looking for. Let's work smarter, not harder. When we get the head (man) healed, he starts taking care of his own body and then meeting the needs of his wife and children.

When you change a man you change the family. When you change a family, you change a community, which changes the city, which changes a state, which changes our nation and impacts our world!

I believe **Ezra 3:11 – 12** is a prophetic word for the move of God today – **"And they sang together by course in praising and giving thanks unto the Lord; because he is good, for his mercy and endureth forever toward Israel. And all the people shouted with a great shout, when they praised the Lord, because the foundation of this house was laid before their eyes, wept with a loud voice; and**

many shouted aloud for joy."

As the body of Christ focuses its efforts on rescuing in restoring fathers, "God's generals" from the Crusades of the 40's and 50's are rejoicing. You see, they remember the days when a man's word was his bond and the family unit was rarely ever divided. Unfortunately, their childhood memories and ideas of manhood are seldom seen in men today. They have watched in dismay as each passing decade has ushered in a greater epidemic of fatherlessness.

However, now that the foundation of the house is once again been laid before their eyes, they are shouting for joy! They understand the need for fathers and they are praising the Lord that we are reestablishing the standard for manhood. We're building the house of God on a solid foundation – Christ like men.

As Jethro charged Moses, I'm going to charge you today – go find some men and equip them to help lead the way in this strategic hour in which we live. We must commit truths to faithful men who will teach others (II Timothy 2:2). We must reverse the curse, right or wrong, and restore order in a world of chaos. We must build men and raise sons! We must **"Take Our Place!"**

God, I'll always miss my hero... Dr. Edwin Louis Cole.

G.F. and Rose Watkins are the founders and Senior Pastors of PowerHouse Church in Katy, TX. Their vision to restore men, resurrect the family, and reach the nations through the vehicle of the local church led them to a ground-breaking development- the **MANCHURCH Strategy.**

The end-time plan is having worldwide impact on pastors, leaders, and believers of all denominations and cultures. The National Coalition of Men's Ministry named Pastor Watkins the "2002 Emerging Leader of the Year."

For more information regarding Pastor Watkins and the ministries he oversees please visit one of the following websites:

www.PowerHouseChurch.tv

www.IntenseMen.com

www.JordanRanch.org

www.dangerousgames.org

CPSIA information can be obtained at www.ICGtesting.com
Printed in the USA
LVOW13s0016090514

385015LV00001B/4/P